TREES
OF
RIGHTEOUSNESS

"The planting of Yahweh, that He might be glorified." Isaiah 61:3

By

Abby Gail

Xulon
PRESS

Trees of Righteousness
"The planting of Yahweh, that He might be glorified." Isaiah 61:3
by Abby Gail

Printed in the United States of America

ISBN 978-1-60477-855-7

Unless otherwise indicated, Bible quotations are taken from The Holy Bible: KJV, (Oral Roberts Evangelistic Association, Inc., Copyright © 1981), and The Mom's Devotional Bible, NIV: (Zondervan Publishing House, Copyright © 1966), and The Restoration of Original Sacred Name Bible: (Basis of the Rotherham Version, Copyright © 1976, Revised by Missionary Dispensary Bible Research, 5th Edition, Copyright © 1977), and The Sacred Scriptures: Bethel Edition, Premier Publication: (Assemblies of Yahweh, Copyright © 1981), and The Old Testament of the Jerusalem Bible: (Darton, Longman & Todd, Ltd., and Doubleday & Company, Inc., Copyright © 1966) quotations by publishers.

This is a work representing stories and Bible doctrine in poetry. The Life Reflections' characters, places and incidents are the author's creation and/or anonymously written and any resemblance to any actual persons, living or dead, events or locales may be coincidental.

1. Religion 2. Poetry 3. Life Reflections 4. Biblical
Photograph - by author

www.xulonpress.com

To Marie,
You are precious
in Our creator's sight.
Thanks for your support.
Abby Gail "2008"

DEDICATION

This book is dedicated to
Our Heavenly Father
YHWH
And our Savior,
YAHSHUA

May the poems and reflections
Provide clarity and comfort.

PREFACE

In this book of poems and reflections, YHWH or Yahweh is used to acknowledge the Creator by His Holy name. This is strange for many believers of the Bible. We are use to acknowledging and using names we were taught. However, you will begin to understand the importance of the Creator's holy name as you read this book.

When Adam and Eve were created, our Heavenly Father communed with them in the Garden of Eden. By trusting Satan, who said they would not, 'surely die,' they disobeyed the Creator and were banished from this earthly paradise wherein was the Tree of Life. (Genesis 3:22) The price for sinning was death. Unlike in the Garden of Eden, Adam and Eve gradually began to get old and eventually died. However, the salvation plan was in place before the fall of Adam and Eve. Our loving Heavenly Father knew they would fall and because of His love and mercy made a way for the restoration of mankind through His only begotten son, Yahshua. Our Savior, Yahshua, is the unblemished Lamb as described in scripture. His sinless blood sacrifice redeemed us to the position of righteous sons and daughters of the Almighty.

Many historical details have been lost throughout the ages. Israel, the lost sheep, was chosen to be a witness of the Creator's love for mankind. For centuries, mankind has been lied to, deceived, and persecuted while consistent attempts were made to keep them in the dark and away from the Creator's holy truths. However, many truths are in open view and through the awesome power of prayer, action and faith, our Heavenly Father directs His children to find these truths. The Savior said we will have a Comforter, the Holy Spirit, who will guide us in all truths. Our Heavenly Father takes great pleasure in answering His children's prayers. His word says, "For we do not wrestle against flesh and blood, but against principalities, against powers, against the rulers of the darkness of this age." (Ephesians 6:12) As we first seek His Kingdom and His righteousness, we will do marvelous things to His glory; and whatever we ask in His son, Yahshua's name, He will do it. The Creator's name is powerful. Scripture states there's no other name whereby we may be saved, therefore, it is important to know His name. Yet, our Heavenly Father makes ways of escape for His loving children to serve Him in spirit and in truth. Scripture reveals, when we are ignorant, our Heavenly Father winks at it. However, when we learn and understand our Creator's commands, but continue in ways contrary to His will, then it is sin. He also tells us, if we lack wisdom to ask Him, and He will give it to us generously. But we must ask in faith and have no doubt. Wisdom comes by hearing the Word. When we read the Bible and meditate on the words, our faith increases. Without faith it is impossible to please our wonderful Creator.

The Creator used the name YHWH, (Tetragrammaton is the four letter word that represents the Creator's sacred name) to identify Himself to the Hebrew nation. In the Hebrew alphabet, each letter has a sound and meaning. Each letter in the Creator's name is pronounced as follows: Y=Yod, H=Hey, W=Wav, H=Hey. Yod Hey Wav Hey is the truest and direct name used by the Creator. Mankind used the four consonants and added vowels to give a more pronounceable form as Yahweh. When the Savior walked the earth, He was called by the name, Yahshua.

There was a period when our Creator revealed His name to the Hebrew forefathers because they did not know it. Names were seen as indicators of one's character, function or destiny. Abram's name was changed to Abraham. His characteristic was faith, because he reverenced the presence of YHWH and believed Him. The patriarchs feared the Creator's name and believed it was too sacred to be spoken aloud. The Hebrew nation was taught to reverence the Creator's name so meticulously that they would not utter His sacred name, YHWH. Even before Abraham's time men were in awe of the Creator's name and understood to use it in any manner to dishonor Him was a grievous and unforgivable sin known as blasphemy.

Thinking they were not sinning against the Creator, scholars changed His name to Lord, which in Hebrew is Adonai, Adonay or Adhonai. They thought by using this substitute, it implied they maintained the closest union with Him without using His holy name. These spiritual leaders failed to realize the removal of YHWH's holy name was equal to extinguishing Him as Creator.

As the Bible was translated, the title, God was placed in the scripture. There are many man made gods that have names to identify themselves. Such gods as Meni, meaning god of good luck; Nibhaz, whose image in the form of a dog was made and worshiped by the Avites when the Samaritan race was being formed (II King 17:31); Nisroch, a deity worshipped in Nineveh; Baal was a Phoenician deity know also as Lord; Elohim was substituted by the Assyrian deity Gawd or God in English, meaning deity of fortune; and Zeus is the sky god. These are just a few of the pagan deities that have actually ascribed and been substituted for the benevolent Creator's holy name.

Scripture admonished the children of Israel to destroy the names of their deities from under heaven. The Creator's holy name, Yod Hey Wav Hey / YHWH, is being restored (Deuteronomy 7:24). Do not be fearful of those who are able to destroy the body, but fear the Creator, Who's able to destroy both the body and soul.

May your quest for biblical truths as you read YHWH's holy name in the following pages increase your desire to draw closer as He reveals the importance of His name. Many in darkness will begin to study for themselves. (Eph. 5:6-10) The journey will be priceless. Lost sheep seeking Him, will hear His voice. (John 10:27) Scripture tells us to seek and we shall find. When we ask anything in the Savior's name, He will do it and provide for our every need. (1 John 14:13-14)

Therefore, if Baal is god serve him, but if YHWH is, then serve Him. Choose today, whom you will serve. (1 King 18:21)

Abby Gail

INTRODUCTION

During a challenging period in my life, I began searching for places to visit where I could renew my relationship with the Almighty. I was looking for a place of peace, rest and health restoration. After much prayer and research, I decided to spend two weeks at a health retreat called, *Times of Refreshing*. This haven of rest, located in the Blue Ridge Mountain area of Blairsville, Georgia, is where the Creator led me. Director, Shelem and his devoted wife, Diane, work together with a wonderful staff to make *Times of Refreshing* a spiritual retreat for their guests. At the end of the first six days everybody were feeling refreshed from the week's activities. On the Sabbath day, after worship, the guests and staff went to a nearby state park to walk and to behold the beauty of nature. The waterfalls were breathtaking. We enjoyed ourselves as we walked the paths and listened to soothing sounds of nature around us. As we ventured down the mountainous steps, I turned to view the splendor of a waterfall. As I turned, my foot slipped on a damp step resulting in an ankle fracture. Everyone stopped to assist, pray and later sang as we waited for the forest ranger and transportation to the hospital. I knew my ankle was broken, yet I was at peace. I've learned through my relationship with our Creator that He makes no mistakes, and this accident was not really about me. Still, I wondered what the Creator's purpose was for me to be laid up for months with a broken ankle. All I knew was that I trusted Him.

I often thought I would write a book. Maybe the book would be about life skills or stories for children, but not poetry. Writing poems was something I rarely did. While recuperating, the words began to flow and I would type the words before they were forgotten. My laptop was close, and to my amazement, this book was being born. It is my desire to write about topics others can relate to. One morning while reading the Bible, my eyes focused on the book of Isaiah. As I read Isaiah 61:1-3, I knew immediately the book's title would be, "Trees of Righteousness." Eight months later I returned to *Times of Refreshing* capturing a breathtaking photograph of trees with the background of the Blue Ridge Mountains. There is no greater love than that of our Creator. Every believer must trust in His unfailing love. He is merciful and expresses His love in ways we may not always understand, but the results are always for our good. Experiences from various sources and/or ideas have been the springboard for the poems written within.

Prayerfully this volume of poems will bless you as the Holy Spirit draws you closer to our Creator, YHWH, and our Blessed Savior, Yahshua. May you be encouraged to live and labor for Him.

Peace and Blessings,

Abby Gail

ACKNOWLEDGEMENT

It is with humble gratitude that I acknowledge individuals who helped me with uncommon generosity. If I have inadvertently omitted anyone's name, I hope my appreciation was expressed in person. No matter where you were at the creation of this book, your input is appreciated.

Jill Walker, thanks for taking time from your busy schedule to encourage and proofread this work. I thank your family for generously sharing you.

Times of Refreshing staff, thanks for taking wonderful care of me in the Blue Ridge Mountain. Olivette, your unselfish care during my healing is ever appreciated.

To my supportive network of friends, and you know who you are, thanks for being just wonderful! You were never too busy to listen to my poems, encourage or pray with me along this poetic journey.

To Patricia Harris and staff at the *Edge Connection*, thanks for your support and opening your doors for consultations.

To Lorine Bellamy, thanks for your assistance during the final stages of this project. Lee Fitzpatrick, I am grateful for your expertise.

To my birth and church family, you are very special. Continue to trust our Savior and Creator's unfailing love. His son, Yahshua, is the way.

To my wonderful son, Shawn, I am proud to be called mother by you and expect great things of you for the glory of YHWH. Thanks for your love and encouragement. Your family is blessed. RAB and TC, you are my precious gifts.

Abby Gail

TABLE OF CONTENT

SECTION 1

"Yahweh said to Moses, Come up to Me on the mountain and stay here, and I will give you the tablets of stone, with the law and commands I have written for their instruction."

Exodus 24:12

COMMANDMENTS

**"Our Creator's perfect heart,
Reaches out to you and me,
Showering His perfect peace,
When we trust, obey,
And believe."**

Abby Gail

WORSHIP ME

How can you say you worship Me,
When you bow and kneel to things made or seen,
Nothing shall be worshipped in place of Me,
I am jealous and demand exclusive loyalty,
I am the Creator of all things.

I freed you from Egypt's bondage and poverty,
To abandon every idol made or seen,
So you will love, honor, and worship only Me,
I am jealous and demand exclusive loyalty,
I am the Creator of all things.

Be not deceived by traditions of man,
To worship idols, people, or anything seen,
Dishonors your Creator and I am not pleased,
I am jealous and demand exclusive loyalty,
I am the Creator of all things.

Had I chosen to be represented visibly,
I'd commune with you as I did Adam and Eve,
Yet, you worship idols and say they represent Me,
I am jealous and demand exclusive loyalty,
I am the Creator of all things.

You idolize whatever you stubbornly please,
Imagination in worship represents your own creativity,
Your pictures and emblems I vehemently despise,
I am jealous and demand exclusive loyalty,
I am the Creator of all things.

I command you to exclusively worship Me,
Not things in the heavens, the waters, or in between,
Yet you worship your things and call them Me,
I am jealous and demand exclusive loyalty,
I am the Creator of all things.

Idol worship is not the service I deserve,
Yet generations still follow traditions of man,
By using objects to represent My Sovereignty,
I am jealous and demand exclusive loyalty,
I am the Creator of all things.

All of My commands you must seriously take,
Do not be like heathens that always imitate,
Read the Word and seek My invisible face,
I am jealous and demand exclusive loyalty,
I am the Creator of all things.

Sinners who refuse to honor Me,
Through the third and forth generations,
Will their children's bondage be,
I am jealous and demand exclusive loyalty,
I am the Creator of all things.

My dear children don't be deceived,
You are justified and sanctified by My mercy,
Obedient hearts yielded I bless and set free,
I am jealous and demand exclusive loyalty,
I am the Creator of all things.

So, how can you say you worship Me,
When you bow and kneel to things made or seen,
Nothing shall be worshipped in place of Me,
I am jealous and demand exclusive loyalty,
I am the Creator of all things.

SPLENDOR OF HIS NAME

Why don't you call Him by His name,
And not use titles that are universally the same?
Our Creator, Father, Savior and King,
Is Worthy to be called by the splendor of His name.

Why do you say He is my God,
And curse and bless in the same word god?
Our Creator, Father, Savior and King,
Is Worthy to be called by the splendor of His name.

We know even Satan has a name,
Called Lucifer in heaven he was so vain,
Our Creator, Father, Savior and King,
Is Worthy to be called by the splendor of His name.

Idols and deities have their names,
Yet we use titles for our Creator universally the same,
Our Creator, Father, Savior and King,
Is Worthy to be called by the splendor of His name.

Using titles make His name ineffective to our shame,
And devalues His holy and sovereign name,
Our Creator, Father, Savior and King,
Is Worthy to be called by the splendor of His name.

Satan confuses our worshipping,
But the Creator knows our hearts are clean,
Our Creator, Father, Savior and King,
Is Worthy to be called by the splendor of His name.

His Holy name's been changed and lost,
But He cradles our names in His every thought.
Our Creator, Father, Savior and King,
Is Worthy to be called by the splendor of His name.

As nations begin to honor His name,
There's joy in knowing, it's an offering,
Our Creator, Father, Savior and King,
Is Worthy to be called by the splendor of His name.

Name recognition provides intimacy,
And closeness beyond what we could ever see.
Our Creator, Father, Savior and King,
Is Worthy to be called by the splendor of His name.

With mercy He sees our human hearts,
He hears our prayers and enlightens our thoughts,
Our Creator, Father, Savior and King,
Is Worthy to be called by the splendor of His name.

Yod Hey Wav Hey is our King,
His cost for wisdom is absolutely free.
Our Creator, Father, Savior and King,
Is Worthy to be called by the splendor of His name.

YHWH is worthy of honor and praise,
Rejoice and sing unto His holy and sovereign name.
Our Creator, Father, Savior and King,
Is Worthy to be called by the splendor of His name.

ALLELUYAH

Alleluyah...All praise to our Heavenly Father,
Alleluyah...All praise to our Heavenly King,
Alleluyah...All praise to our Creator,
Alleluyah...Who has given us all things.

Alleluyah...Let us humbly come before Him,
Alleluyah...Let us honor Him and sing,
Alleluyah...Let us bow down before Him,
Alleluyah...Praising our merciful King.

Alleluyah...He deserves to be worshipped,
Alleluyah...He deserves to be praised,
Alleluyah...He deserves to be honored,
Alleluyah...To be called by His holy name.

Alleluyah...The Son's name is in the Father's,
Alleluyah...The scripture reveals His name to use,
Alleluyah...Yahshua is the Son's holy name,
Alleluyah...So what is the Father's name too?

Alleluyah...The Father's name has been taken away,
Alleluyah...His name has been brought to nought,
Alleluyah...We sing unto Them and unknowingly,
Alleluyah...Yahweh and Yahshua's names we exalt.

REMEMBER

You told us to remember,
You knew some would forget,
You created the world in six days,
On the seventh day You told us to rest.

The seventh day is the Sabbath,
The Sabbath of our Creator and King,
When He said cease from all our labor,
Not even humans or cattle shall do anything.

As we read the story of creation,
Each day was divided and fixed,
The evening and morning distinguished each day,
No clocks were around for us to be tricked.

We are to continue our Creator's example,
Diligently work from the first day through the sixth,
Cease from our work and rest on the Sabbath,
The only day He made holy and blessed.

You told us to remember,
You knew some would forget,
You created the world in six days,
On the seventh day You told us to rest.

When we honor His holy Sabbath,
We acknowledge love for our Heavenly King,
For only He can renew our spirit,
As we rest in His Sabbath day springs.

Sabbath begins on the sixth day at sunset,
It ends at sunset on the seventh,
If we continue in obedience to His commands,
On the Sabbath we'll worship Him in heaven.

You told us to remember,
You knew some would forget,
You created the world in six days,
On the seventh day You told us to rest.

With every command our Creator has,
Satan despises and counterfeits,
Don't be surprised just read His word,
And the history books will also confess.

Don't be confused the worship day was changed,
It was in 321 A.D.
A Roman Emperor named Constantine,
Changed the Creator's worship day to Sun-day.

Constantine banished worship on the Sabbath,
Forced worship on the venerable day of the Sun,
To refuse to conform to a new worship day,
Lives were not spared and many hand to run.

You told us to remember,
You knew some would forget,
You created the world in six days,
On the seventh day You told us to rest.

Like a bride desiring to please her love,
We should keep all the Creator's commands,
If you have doubts study for yourself,
And allow the Creator to guide your hands.

The Sabbath day is still holy,
The crucified Savior rested in His tomb,
He rose on the first day of the week to finish his mission,
And not a change in the Sabbath did He presume.

You told us to remember,
You knew some would forget,
You created the world in six days,
On the seventh day You told us to rest.

Revelations 22:14 says,
"Blessed are they that do His Commandments,
That they may have right to the tree of life,
And may enter in through the gates into the city"

Obedience in love to all His commands,
Is the narrow road into His majestic city,
For the road is wide that leads us astray,
And following it would be a pity.

You told us to remember,
You knew some would forget,
You created the world in six days,
On the seventh day You told us to rest.

HONOR YOUR FATHER AND MOTHER

Honor your father and mother,
Is a command written by the Creator's hand,
When you obediently yield to their earthly positions,
You're honoring the Creator's plan.

Some only have one father and mother,
Just respect and appreciate who they are,
Others may have more parents than you,
Blood related or adopted near or far.

Honor your father and mother,
Can sometimes seem difficult to do,
Constantly pray for them even when you think,
They're not doing right by you.

Honor your father and mother,
The Creator judges those with your care,
When you pray and trust for the good in them,
He'll shower blessings because of your prayers.

Some parents may forsake their children,
But the Creator never, ever will,
When you need to feel His living touch,
He will provide whether you're healthy or ill.

Whether you have righteous parents,
Or whether they're caught up in sin,
It's not for you to judge your parents,
Your responsibility is to always honor them.

Honor your father and mother,
Whether you're young or whether you're old,
The relationship of honoring your parents,
Provides nourishment to the saving of your own soul.

DO NOT MURDER

We are cautioned not to commit murder,
Yet most are guilty of this,
To kill a person or their good name,
Is called murder and we must desist.

Some people hate within their hearts,
Whether they're jealous, scorned or rejected,
Release the feeling and be set free,
So your life may become a blessing.

When the Heavenly Father controls your life,
There's no need for you to worry,
Satan had to ask for permission to hinder Job,
Yet scripture said Job's trust never once varied.

Whether you are the victim or the perpetrator,
The sad result is at each family's door,
Not to commit murder in words or deed,
Is possible, if that is what you're praying for.

ADULTERY

You've been joined together,
As husband and wife,
Anointed as one,
For the rest of your life.

Depend on Yahweh,
Be true to your vows,
Continue to shower,
The love you show now.

He's the head and protector,
Specializing in love,
A worthy investment,
Redeemed from above.

She'll honor your day,
And make it so sweet,
Like living in heaven,
A home of joy and peace.

Your marriage is sacred,
It is holy and blessed,
You are both responsible,
To resist adulterous tests.

If either of you venture,
From your wedding sheets,
By lusting upon another,
Or consummating your heat.

Don't be deceived,
Your sinful joy won't last,
It's temporary pleasure,
To separate your paths.

Stolen moments of pleasure,
Is deceitful to your mate,
Dishonors your Creator,
And exhibits internal hate.

IT'S STEALING

Stealing has many faces,
Can you relate to the following?
To take what belongs to another,
Is stealing their property.
To deprive joy to others in need,
Is stealing away moments of serenity.
Not giving an honest hour for your work,
Is stealing what you promised to do.
To lie when others trust in your word,
Is stealing confidence in what you say is true.
Disappointing others who depend on you,
Is stealing their belief in your words.
Making promises you don't plan to keep,
Is stealing one's hopes or dreams.
To hold on to someone you don't truly love,
Is stealing their freedom to love anew.
To say you love but your actions are contrary,
Is stealing time and trust in your relationship.
To abuse and mistreat children in your care,
Is stealing their precious childhood.
Not loving your spouse in word and deed,
Is stealing promises from your marriage vows.
Preventing a child from spending time with grandparents,
Is stealing values, memories and their feeling of security.
To use children as ponds between their parents,
Is stealing children's fragile self-esteem.
To neglect to help others in times of need,
Is stealing an opportunity to serve them well.
To waste when you can protect and conserve,
Is stealing opportunities to beautify for others to see.
To disregard the value of another living soul,
Is stealing an opportunity of showing humanity.
To work so much family time is neglected,
Is stealing time from those you're entrusted to teach.
To believe and not teach nor worship with your family,

Is stealing time to be used wisely for souls of eternity.
'Do Not Steal,' may be a short command,
But the meaning goes on, and on, and on.
Stealing is...

DON'T LIE!

Don't lie to Me and say that you love Me,
Don't lie to Me and say that you care,
Don't lie to Me and say I'm your witness,
Liars are not welcome here!

Don't lie to them and think I'll condone it,
Don't lie to them because you have no fear,
Don't lie to them and say you are like Me,
Liars are not welcome here!

Don't lie to them to gain popularity,
Don't lie to them and cause them to sin,
Don't lie to them being cleverly deceitful,
Liars are not welcome here!

Don't lie to them to draw them unto you,
Don't lie to them to sleep in their beds,
Don't lie to them for self-gratification,
Liars are not welcome here!

Don't lie to them saying you're an honest leader,
Don't lie to them saying, "May God strike me dead,"
Don't lie to them distorting My scriptures,
Liars are not welcome here!

Don't lie to them to cause their confusion,
Don't lie to them destroying trust in My word,
Don't lie to them when you're not converted,
Liars are not welcome here!

Don't lie to Me and say you've been faithful,
Don't lie to Me professing souls you have saved,
Don't lie to Me expecting to enter My kingdom,
Liars are not welcome here!

FALSE WITNESS

To bear false witness against a neighbor,
Is lying when the truth should be told,
Choices we make show one's true character,
And we'll reap whatever we sow.

To be truthful in dealings with neighbors,
We must treat others with respect and honesty,
To be the recipient of lies is painful,
Especially if it's from friends or family.

In the court of law, we swear to tell the truth,
Yet some still bear false witness against others,
And if falsely convicted for a crime or deed,
The result can destroy the life or youth of another.

A person's word should be his bond,
When others will lie, being honest shows strength,
We'll someday stand before the heavenly courts,
And hear those words recorded from our lips.

Will you be found guilty of this offense,
Or will your false witness case be dismissed?
Come before the Savior's throne of forgiveness,
And do not dare become a false witness.

LONGINGS

Some desire the wealth that others possess,
Or long for a neighbor's spouse,
Some desire the expensive home or car,
That brings prestige to a neighbor's life.

Some desire to be famous to obtain security,
Or to be the only one at the top of their game,
Some desire the pleasure of being well known,
So others will idolize their fame.

Some desire their neighbor's wealth or power,
And will gain by deception to fulfill their greed,
Some desire servants that others have,
And begrudge owners for a life of luxury.

Some desire things they can't afford to buy,
Spending money to shop until they drop,
When accumulations fail to satisfy their wants,
They build bigger barns to enclose their lots.

Some desire to be the talk of the town,
They live to attract the attention of others,
Some desire compliments and flattering tongues,
Yet will not give to the need of a brother.

Some desire things which temporarily satisfies,
And after acquired the excitement's no longer known,
Some covet whatever a neighbor may own,
And give each breath to keep up with the Joneses.

Our material desires are never satisfied,
After obtaining we search for other gains,
Yet there's a longing ingrained in each of us,
That will alleviate our selfish shame.

'Do Not Covet,' is a command we must obey,
When our desire for materialism struggles to come first,
When we seek a relationship with our awesome Creator,
Our desire for Him will fulfill your every thirst.

THE TEN COMMANDMENTS
EXODUS CHAPTER 20

And Yahweh spoke all these words, saying, I am Yahweh your Elohim which have brought you out of the land of Egypt (a country occupying the north-eastern angle of Africa), **out of the house of bondage** (external control; slavery).

I

You shall have no other Elohim (God, as used in the Hebrew text), **before Me.**

II

You shall not make unto (for) **yourself any graven** (carved or sculptured) **idol** (form), **or any likeness** (picture or portrait) **of anything that is in the heaven above, or that is in the earth beneath, or that is in the water under the earth:**

You shall not bow (bend) **down yourself to them nor serve** (worship) **them: For I Yahweh Your Elohim am a jealous** (demanding exclusive loyalty) **Elohim, visiting the iniquity** (wickedness or sin) **of the fathers upon the children unto** (up to or until) **the third and fourth generation** (offspring; a grandfather, father and son are three generations) **of them that hate me; and showing mercy** (favor, pity or reward) **unto thousands of them that love me, and keep my commandments.**

III

You shall not take away (abolish; get rid of) **the name of Yahweh your Elohim to bring it to naught** (no value or not at all). **Yahweh will not hold him guiltless that takes away His name to bring it to nought.**

IV

Remember (recall, not forget) **the Sabbath Day** (the 7th day of the week set aside for worship) **to keep it holy** (pure, sacred, reverenced, set apart).

Six days shall you labour (labor, exert oneself, toil) **and do all your work;**

But the seventh day is the Sabbath Day of Yahweh, your Elohim: in it you shall not do any work; not you, nor your son, nor your daughter, nor your man servant, nor your maid servant, nor your cattle (animals), **nor a stranger that is within your gates** (home or property);

For in six days Yahweh made heaven and earth, the sea and all that in them is and rested the seventh day: wherefore Yahweh blessed (made consecrated; sacred; holy; sanctified) **the Sabbath-Day and hollowed** (honored holy, sacred) **it.**

V

Honor (respect) **your father and your mother; that your days may be long on the land that Yahweh give to you.**

VI

You shall not commit murder (kill).

VII

You shall not commit adultery (sex with someone when you are married; lust for someone).

VIII

You shall not steal (take secretly).

IX

You shall not bear false (not true or lie) **witness** (a person who saw) **against your neighbour** (others or people you know).

X

You shall not covet (desire, crave) **your neighbour's house, his wife, nor his man servant, nor his maid servant, nor his ox** (cattle), **nor his ass** (donkey), **nor anything that belongs to your neighbour.**

SECTION 2

"Because he loves me," says Yahweh, "I will rescue him; I will protect him, for he acknowledges my name. He will call upon me, and I will answer him; I will be with him in trouble, I will deliver him and honor him. With long life will I satisfy him and show him My salvation."

Psalm 91:14-16

LIFE REFLECTIONS

**"This chapter of reflections,
Reveals His loving grace.
The lives within He cherish,
And draws in His embrace."**

Abby Gail

IT'S NOT ABOUT ME

The first lesson that You taught me Father,
As I knelt down on my knees,
And asked You to lead and guide me was,
It's about Your will, and not about me.

You placed the desire in my heart,
To read Your word from the old to the new,
The Testament scripture came to life for me,
In ways I never knew.

The weekend this reading journey began,
Each day I'd read Deuteronomy, Chapter 8,
This powerful chapter beginning with the word "All,"
Tells how to please You, and to read it, I could not hesitate.

For the whole month of September,
Each day, maybe once, twice, or more,
I would meditate upon Deuteronomy, Chapter 8,
Gaining insights from the scriptures as my spirit soared.

Randomly I'd read each book in the Old Testament,
Yet nothing happens by chance when the Father leads,
Although I've read many parts of the Bible before,
The lessons are the same, it's about You and not about me.

Let me back up for a minute that I may be clear,
At a conference service in Atlanta, Georgia that week,
The man was asked to read a scripture verse for service,
Then was immediately asked by the host if he preached.

The brother quite candidly obliged to preach,
And with the Holy Spirit he was definitely prepared,
He knew immediately the book and chapter he'd seek,
And Deuteronomy, Chapter 8, began my spiritual love affair.

With hearing ears and seeing eyes,
Sitting still as a river of tears flowed from each side,
My heart was touched by these precious words,
"All My commandments, ye shall do," And I had to abide.

I returned home at the end of the conference,
The Father's words in my heart had been renewed,
His words were sharper than any two edged sword,
Reading the complete Bible was something I had to do.

In the secular world to obtain a degree,
Experience proves by reading books in their entirety,
And tested for understanding and clarity,
An ace for the grade we'd most likely receive.

If we say we love our Creator,
We must take the time with Him to commune,
By prayerfully reading His scriptural love letters,
His wisdom and understanding is freely given too.

Love and serve are action words,
To say you love and not act on it is being false,
Our Heavenly Father never lies,
Keeping His commands strengthen our hearts.

When the Holy Spirit guides,
You don't often know what you'll do,
The Holy Spirit placed me in a fasting and prayer mode,
To encourage others with my spiritual breakthrough.

The darts of Satan were fiercely on attack,
Don't be surprised when it happens to you,
When you go on the Creator's spiritual journey,
Satan gets upset because he fears losing you.

There is so much I'd love to share with you,
But let me go back to the Holy Book,
It's the beginning of my renewed spiritual journey,
And not one chapter from reading it, I forsook.

As I read the New Testament of the Bible,
Was touched as I read how the Savior cried,
The night before He died on Calvary saying,
"Father, not My will, but Thine."

I completed the Bible in less than a year,
This time returning from Atlanta with a group of kids,
Was elated sharing on the bus with adult friends,
That I'd just completed the Bible from beginning to end.

The first lesson that You taught me Father,
As I knelt down on my knees,
And asked You to lead and guide me was,
It's about Your will, and not about me.

TO MY CREATOR
IF...

If I could see beyond the stars,
And share Your stories to those near and far.

If I could reach beyond myself,
And write to souls that need Your help.

If the words I write could encourage others,
Words that strengthen, build and uplift my brothers.

If these words would soften the hearts of men,
Without them having to pay the ultimate cost for sin.

If my desire to write has meaning in this life,
Then and only then, it is worth the fight.

If I could look into Your brilliant eyes,
Father, maybe, just maybe then, I would be wise.

MY FAVORITE

You are my favorite Father,
The true love I adore,
You've been a lifetime blessing,
Of all I've asked, You've given more.

You bring forth sunlight to the flowers,
For the growing grass You spread forth dew,
The blissfulness in nature,
Allows men's heart to renew.

How can I express my love assuredly?
How can I show my love for You?
It's in the stillness of the morning,
That I awake and speak to You.

ALMIGHTY FATHER

Almighty Father,
Fill me with your love,
Lead me in Your righteousness,
From Heaven's portal above,
Fill me with Your Spirit,
Ever mindful of Your grace,
Striving for humility,
As I run this earthly race.

Almighty Father,
Teach me how to live,
Fill my heart with kindness,
And the ability to truly forgive,
Guide my words and actions,
Place Your pureness in my heart,
For my concern is to please You,
For the love lessons You have taught.

Almighty Father,
Grant understanding and grace,
Teach me things through Your eyes,
So little children will seek Your face,
Give me strength and compassion,
Knowing You desire to save the lost,
By lifting up the righteous Savior,
Who for all mankind paid the cost.

DEEP INSIDE OF ME

Who can give me joy and gladness,
Fill my working days of sadness?
It doesn't matter what you see,
I know the answer deep inside of me.

Who can pardon all my sins,
And give me life renewed again?
It doesn't matter what you see,
I know the answer deep inside of me.

Who can I depend on now,
When all the chips are looking down?
It doesn't matter what you see,
I know the answer deep inside of me.

Who will protect and fight for me,
When others scatter, afraid to be free?
It doesn't matter what you see,
I know the answer deep inside of me.

Who will speak for me in court,
When I no longer have a voice?
It doesn't matter what you see,
I know the answer deep inside of me.

Who will comfort my tears and sorrows,
As each new day brings brighter tomorrows?
It doesn't matter what you see,
I know the answer deep inside of me.

Who has prepared a place for me,
A mansion where I will live for eternity?
It doesn't matter what you see,
I know the answer deep inside of me.

So take the journey, have faith and believe,
Our Heavenly Father will provide your every need.
It doesn't matter what you see,
He is the answer deep inside of you and me.

FATHER OF RIGHTEOUSNESS

Father of Righteousness,
As we walk this narrow road,
Shield, guide, protect us,
And make us truly whole.
Empowered with Your Spirit,
Of goodwill and righteousness,
Lead, teach, and try our hearts,
As we walk in Your footsteps.

Father of Righteousness,
As ambassadors for You,
Let others see our good works,
And bow to worship You.
May we honor and obey,
All of Your commands,
In our strength we'll fail,
But You will lift our hands.

Father of Righteousness,
When discouraged or in pain,
May we offer praise to You,
Like the rainbow after the rain,
Sharing our trials with others,
All victories coming from You,
Trusting without seeking to know,
Your methods of guiding us through.

Father of Righteousness,
Obeying is difficult indeed,
Like selfish little children,
We want the things we see,
Our spirit may be willing,
But our flesh is much too weak,
We think now is the appointed time,
To satisfy what we momentarily seek.

Father of Righteousness,
Today we humbly pray,
Give us honorable mentors,
To guide us through our days,
Believers to help us focus,
On how You brought us through,
Your children of faith and trust,
Who believes what You say, You'll do.

Father of Righteousness,
Help us to hold onto all that's good,
To consciously make wise choices,
By Your wisdom, knowledge and truth,
For those that truly trust in You,
Knows all Your works are good,
And only in Your appointed time,
Will provide the results that it should.

Father of Righteousness,
Our awesome Father and friend,
Strengthen the minds of Your dear ones,
Determined to be obedient until the end,
As we escape Satan's alluring traps,
His lies that's detrimental to our souls,
May we continue to seek Your face,
And Your peace we shall behold.

WITHOUT A DREAM

Without a dream
No man lives
Without a dream
No one cares
Without a dream
Nothing's forgiven
Without a dream
Why are we here?

Without a dream
Women are lonely
Without a dream
Men are in despair
Without a dream
Children aren't loving
Without a dream
Our nation doesn't care.

Without a dream
Life is a whisper
Without a dream
Songs are never heard
Without a dream
Thoughts become vapors
Without a dream
Civilizations will disappear!

GRATITUDE

Maybe you changed our diapers,
Maybe you washed our face,
Maybe you gave us good food to eat,
Maybe you taught us grace.

Maybe you prayed for our protection,
Maybe you gave us wonderful advice,
Maybe you taught us how to be strong,
Maybe you taught us what's wrong and right.

Whatever you've done during our tender years,
To shape us into whom we have become,
We want to take the time right now,
To thank you for all you've done.

Our prayer is,
"For all you've done for us,
And what you often do,
May your blessings be greater,
And returned ten-fold to you."

HOW BLESSED!

How blessed I am to have a Father,
Who loves me each and every day.
A Heavenly Father Who cares about me,
As I seek Him each dawn and pray.

How blessed I am to know the comfort,
Of a Father's strong and gentle love.
Strong arms that protect me from danger,
His gentle touch when I desire an earthly hug.

How blessed I am to know my Father,
Will work out my problems bad or good.
Though I've continued to make a bunch of mistakes,
His outrageous love draws me as nothing else could.

How blessed I am to have a Father,
Who placed love songs of Himself in my heart,
The words and sometimes a melody,
To share with others His creative thoughts.

How blessed I am to know my Father,
Will guide my writing hands,
The words I write are love letters,
Only a sincere heart can understand.

IF I COULD BE

If I could be, more like You,
If I could see, more like You,
If I could lead, more like You,
Then I would be free.

Nothing could prevent me,
No one could resist me,
All my dreams accomplished,
If I could be, more like You.

Although this world's in bondage,
Our children cry for mercy,
On death ears fall their voices,
Yet, their cries You always hear.

If I could love, more like You,
If I could live, more like You,
If I could serve, more like You,
Father, then all Your children would be free.

LOVE ME FOREVER

Love me forever,
Help me to be,
Forever trusting,
Only in Thee.

Love me forever,
Help me to see,
Only through Your eyes
What I should be.

Love me forever,
Make me brand new,
Teach me your knowledge,
Wisdom and truths.

Love me forever,
Always to see,
I'll have a future,
Living with Thee.

MORNING TIL NIGHT

Good morning Heavenly Father,
Please forgive my sins,
May I honor you in righteousness,
As this brand new day begins.

Good afternoon Heavenly Father,
What a blessed and peaceful day,
Showing me Your touching grace,
As I walk each path You pave.

Good evening Heavenly Father,
What joy has filled my heart,
You carried all my burdens away,
And not from me depart.

Good night Heavenly Father,
As I close my eyes to sleep,
Let me dream of You only,
As I rest this night in peace.

IN THE PILLOW OF MY ARMS

In the Pillow of my arms,
I wake up to You.

As I hold the pillow in my embrace,
I wake up to You.

Sweet, secured, and rested,
My dreams are guided by thoughts of You.

I am embraced in Your agape love.
In the pillow of my arms.

I am adored.
I am at peace.
I am fearless.
I am secured.

Always, in the pillow of Your love.

LET THE CHILDREN COME

Let the children come,
They are so precious.
Let the children come,
They will come to Me.
Let the children come,
They're innocent and loving.
Let the children come,
They giggle hilariously.
Let the children come,
They are pure in heart.
Let the children come,
They listen to my stories.
Let the children come,
They bury Me in hugs.
Let the children come,
They believe My words are true.
Let the children come,
They pray in pureness of heart.
Let the children come,
They will dance for me in heaven.
Let the children come,
They fill My arms with love.

INNER CHILD

The inner child in you and me,
May not have always known the way,
Could have been loved and cared for,
Or unappreciated but we're here to stay.

Shielded with others to protect us,
Or putting up walls to secure our hearts,
We've learned to enjoy each moment,
And allowed chaos to elude our inner thoughts.

Be not afraid of the tempests,
Or the daily storms in our lives,
Hold strong to beliefs that are righteous,
And do not cheat our inner peace with this fight.

Live each day to the fullest,
Be prayerful our lives to enjoy,
Let the Master fight our many battles,
When adversities come, give the Creator the floor.

MIRACLE

Born before her time,
A blessing to all who knew her,
Infectious personality and loving smile,
Hearts melt as she came into their presence.

Wisdom from beyond the clouds,
Compassion beyond her years,
Joyful and quite a personality,
Eager to love everyone she met,
In purity she received the love of many.

Purposeful,
Time was too short,
Stricken but not defeated,
Talkative, bubbly and sweet,
Grown up beyond her years,
Yet only the age of five.

Saw Mickey and had the video to share,
Didn't have to wait in Disney's line,
Had very little time,
Her "Make a Wish" come true,
Her mommy, daddy and sister went too.

Never shy about enjoying the moments,
Left joyful memories of love in our hearts,
Even strangers approached her,
Little Miracle had no fear,
And was so much fun from the start.

She fought the fight of cancer,
Chemo did its tiring toll,
Her medication changed her physically,
But her loving personality it could not destroy,
She fought, and fought the cancerous enemy,
Made efforts to win the race of time.

Her spirit was trying to beat death,
But her flesh was much too weak,
She went to sleep in the month of June, 2002,
The sweet, sweet, sleep of death.

Her mother could not be comforted,
Her daddy and her older sister too,
The church was filled to capacity,
She was loved,
And missed by everyone she knew.

Miracle's grandmother was my dear friend,
Who also suffered with cancer for many years,
Was wheeled in the church to say her final good bye,
As many people wiped away their tears.

Miracle looked like a beautiful doll,
In her white casket with stuffed animals,
She was a miracle to have even been born,
A miracle of love in her very short life,
And now a miracle in her death.

My three grandchildren attended Miracle's funeral,
And asked why she had to die so young,
I told them of our Heavenly Father's mercies,
And how Miracle was His joy and delight,
They were sad but understood,
That Miracle is precious in His sight.

The sermon was moving and touched many hearts,
The pastor told them to hold on,
And never each other to forsake,
Not to allow past problems to keep them apart,
As Miracle's father joined her mother to embrace.

As we left the funeral,
I listened to the prompting in my heart,
And knew I had to make a bold call,
The grandchildren would witness another miracle,
To a family member I had not spoken with for so long.

I had written a letter some months before,
But never received a response,
I shared how Satan meant it for evil,
But our Creator allowed it for our good,
When there are problems both parties must meet,
It doesn't matter who's at fault,
The offender and the offended both must humbly retreat.

Made a phone call and returned to my car,
Sharing with my little ones,
How Our Creator restores families,
And repairs things broken or lost,
When we are obedient as the Holy Spirit speaks,
He will give us more than we seek.

So do not hesitate or wait,
When the Holy Spirit guides your fate,
Nothing in this world can bind,
What our Heavenly Father creates.

Miracle's life was very short,
But it was not in vain,
A long life was not her path to take,
But she showered us with love when she came,
And if we learn from her short life,
Just maybe we can do the same.

We do not know how long we'll live,
As we live from day to day,
But when the Holy Spirit speaks,
Defeat your pride and humbly obey.

Miracle's story may seem sad and sweet,
Her goodness no one else could beat,
For love was all she had to give,
Freely given and freely lived.

YOUR HELP

We need Your help, to care for this gift,
We need Your help, before we're undone,
We need Your help, to think before we leap,
We need Your help, before it is ruined.

Without Your help, we'll make wrong choices,
Without Your help, temperance is not won,
Without Your help, our bodies will curse us,
Without your help, all hope will be gone.

Teach us temperance, with each passing hour,
Teach us temperance, for what should be done,
Teach us temperance, in what we choose daily,
Teach us temperance, for the battle to be won.

Show us wisdom, to care for each member,
Show us wisdom, in choices we make,
Show us wisdom, in foods that's sustaining,
Show use wisdom, to evaluate our intake.

Give us understanding, that we may stay healthy,
Give us understanding, to sustain for today,
Give us understanding, to trust in Your wisdom,
Give us understanding, for our bodies You gave.

LAUGH OUT LOUD

Don't get stuck when trials beset you,
Like there's nothing else to do,
Search the scriptures,
Read the message,
Special love letters,
Written just for you.

Laugh out loud,
Smile a lot,
Dance around,
Praise in song,
Hold on firmly,
To all His promises,
You've been delivered,
Before you were born.

You are precious,
Like a flower,
His living water will lift you up,
Words to inspire you,
Your faith will revive you,
Focus only on,
His spiritual truths.

Laugh out loud,
Smile a lot,
Dance around,
Praise in song,
Hold on firmly,
To all His promises,
You've been delivered,
Before you were born.

Praise the Savior,
For your blessings,
For the ways,
He brought you through,
For His love and compassion,
That your hearts,
May be renewed.

Laugh out loud,
Smile a lot,
Dance around,
Praise in song,
Hold on firmly,
To all His promises,
You've been delivered,
Before you were born.

FRIENDSHIPS

A friend sticks closer than a brother,
Acquaintances will come and go,
During times when you need emotional lifts,
True friends will prove their worth in gold.

Man is not an island unto himself,
We depend on others each day,
Friends are near in the good and bad times,
And will honor you along life's way.

To have friends you must be gracious,
Consideration and hospitality goes far,
And making deposits by being good listeners,
True friends will be honest when you call.

Forgiveness is a gift to friendships,
Sometimes trial and error gets in the way,
When willing to forgive and listen to each other,
Friends support you when no one else will stay.

Friends, you are a joy to talk to,
Acquaintances, it was nice to see you smile,
Trials are the test friendships are made of,
And love's the glue that goes the extra mile.

ANGEL KISSES

When I'm starting each new day,
As I kneel to my Creator and pray,
And I take in each new breath,
That's an angel kiss from You.

When I receive a morning call,
From a sister who lives quite far,
And we laugh and share our joys,
That's an angel kiss from You.

When my spirit needs lifting up,
And there's no one here to touch,
And a friendship card arrives,
That's an angel kiss from You.

When I see a brand new mom,
Nursing her newborn, singing a song,
And he clings to her real tight,
That's an angel kiss from You.

When I see little children smile,
As they ride on the merry-go-round,
And they act silly and giggle loud,
That's an angel kiss from You.

When I go to the grocery store,
And someone kindly opens the door,
And they share a gentle smile,
That's an angel kiss from You.

When I travel to countries and places,
Seeing sights and people of other races,
And wonder how lucky I've been,
That's an angel kiss from You.

When I receive a call from a friend,
Asking me for a helping hand,
And I'm able to oblige,
That's an angel kiss from You.

When there's been an accident,
And the pain is only a small percent,
And others comfort, sing and pray,
That's an angel kiss from You.

When I have a healthy diet,
Fruits and vegetables to nourish life,
And my body is healthy and strong,
That's an angel kiss from You.

When friends come to visit me,
Sharing good times and just being free,
And we commune in joy and laughter,
That's an angel kiss from You.

When not feeling my very best,
And all I want to do is rest,
Having friends love and care for me,
That's an angel kiss from You.

When I take time to study Your word,
Seeking wisdom in things I haven't heard,
And I understand a thing or two,
That's an angel kiss from You.

When Your children are being blessed,
As You put them to the test,
And they trust Your holiness,
That's an angel kiss from You.

When I made it through another day,
Whispering words to You of praise,
And You provide my every need,
That's an angel kiss from You.

ALL THESE CHILDREN!

All these children, he said to his wife.
All these children, they disrupted his life.
All these children, he didn't want to have right away.
All these children, her clock was ticking so what the hay.
All these children, were the words he'd sound.
All these children, please cherish their little frowns,
All these children, words I often dread.
All these children, just a few and acted so sad.
All these children, repeated from a generation past.
All these children, how long will this curse last?
All these children, what does he want to do?
All these children, too late for birth control tools.
All these children, he truly loved and cares.
All these children, will bless their golden years.
All these children, will give unconditional love.
All these children, cherish them as our Creator does.
All these children, provide hugs and joyful sounds.
All these children, start looking up and stop looking down.
All these children, you need to find positive things to say.
All these children, change your behavior, seek and pray.

All these children, I'll tell you a story that is true.
All these children, another dad complained before you.
All these children, his only son died and he cried.
All these children, yet he complained about the other five.
All these children, brought him joy as his end drew near.
All these children, sheltered their dad in his golden years.
All these children, please take serious my advice.
All these children, hear what I know to be right.
All these children, and this I know for sure.
All these children, words can build or destroy one's core,
All these children, you can now end this curse.
All these children, future generations don't need to hurt.
All these children, just take some quiet spiritual time.
All these children, and study the Creator's divine mind.
All these children, are your heritage, protection and swords.
All these children, happy is a man with so great a reward.

All these children, be thankful for your heavenly blessings.
All these children, must know your love and not be guessing.
All these children, let our Creator gently remind you.
All these children, will be grown and you'll be without a clue.
All these children, young dad, let these blessed ones know.
All these children, your greatest gifts are these little souls.

HIS LITTLE CHILDREN

The apple of His eye,
Pure and innocent,
Trusting implicitly,
An open slate,
His little Children.

Trusting in their care givers,
Fed by those in charge,
Taught the ideology of others,
So faithful in their trust,
His little Children.

Abused and tormented,
Regarded as inconveniences,
Unappreciated and unloved,
Although lovely, feel ugly,
His little Children.

Emotionally beaten down,
Solitary and afraid,
Mistreated, misunderstood,
Laugh to scorn,
His little Children.

Prays to Him their only hope,
Reads His word to understand,
Learned it's about Him and not them,
Discovers He will fight for them,
His little Children.

Faithful to care for those He love,
Providing for their every need,
They're at peace amongst the storms,
Trusting Him they joyfully sing,
All His little Children.

A CHILD

When I was a child,
I thought as a child,
I acted like a child,
I played like a child,
I was a child, a child of the King.

When I was a parent,
I thought as a parent,
I acted like a parent,
I saved like a parent,
I was a parent, a parent for the King.

When I became a grandparent,
I thought like a grandparent,
I acted like a grandparent,
I prayed like a grandparent,
I was a grandparent, a grandparent for the King.

When I was old and gray,
I couldn't remember many things,
I acted somewhat strange,
I prayed, I prayed, I think I prayed,
I am a child, a child of the King.

IT'S OK

It's ok to cry,
He puts all your tears in a bottle.
It's ok to seek,
Seek Him first and everything will be yours.
It's ok to laugh,
Laughter is good for the soul.
It's ok to speak,
When speaking the words of wisdom.
It's ok to heal,
With His stripes we are healed.
It's ok to forgive,
We're forgiven debts as we forgive others.
It's ok to feel,
In keeping the Commandments we feel no evil thing.
It's ok to live,
Live peacefully with all men.
It's ok to listen,
Listen to the Savior's instructions and live.
It's ok to learn,
Learn to do well; seek judgment.
It's ok to strengthen,
The Creator will strengthen you with His mouth.
It's ok to discern,
Discern both good and evil.
It's ok to fear,
The fear of the Creator is the beginning of wisdom.
It's ok to pray,
Pray one for another.
It's ok to care,
The Creator cares for you.
It's ok to obey,
Obey the commandments and live.

Do something special for others today,
It's ok.

THE PROMPTING

She was engrossed in reading,
A favorite series ending in,
"Love's Unending Legacy,"
Then finally fell asleep,
After taking meds for relief.

She was suddenly awakened,
And prompted to make a call,
To a colleague she would greet,
As they would pass in the hall.

This prompting was unusual,
Neither had time to call,
They worked different shifts,
And were too busy,
To even socialize at all.

Without a reason to call Victory,
She rationalized it was late,
But every time she dozed,
The prompting would not hesitate.

She phoned several times,
Only to get a busy line,
Would fall back to sleep.
But the promptings increased.

When the phone finally rung,
Victory answered the call,
She spoke about the promptings,
And not knowing why she called,
Then to her surprise stated,
"I just called to tell you,
Everything will be alright."

Victory began to sob and said,
The call was an answer to prayer.
She was a new believer,
And with childlike faith,
Prayed earnestly with tears,
Asking if the Savior hears,
To give a sign and not hesitate,
So she would be comforted,
Knowing He cares and relates.

When Victory's phone rang,
As she rose from her knees,
And heard her friend's response,
There was no doubt in her mind,
This was an immediate answer,
To her prayerful and heartfelt plea.

Both ladies were humbled,
And thanked the Father above,
For this wonderful experience,
Of the Savior's unfailing love,

The gift of His eternal grace.
Prompted by the Holy Spirit,
Made this a special night,
Forever in their hearts' embrace.

She finally fell asleep in peace,
And in awe of knowing,
Their faith increased,
When the Savior answered,
The earnest prayer,
Of His precious daughter,
Victory.

KNOWING YOU

Knowing You is loving You,
With all my imperfections shining through,
You've given me hope when I was down,
You've turned my heart and life around.

Knowing You is loving You,
No matter what I say or do,
You've been with me through thick and thin,
Without You where would my life end?

Knowing You is loving You,
Your grace abounds each day anew,
You've never once let me down,
You've turned my thoughts and desires around.

Knowing You is loving You,
A Creator whom I've tried and proved,
When living according to Your will,
What sweet moments You always fulfill.

Knowing You is loving You,
Knowing You is loving You,
What more can I say,
Knowing You Father is loving You.

MAKE TIME FOR ME

Said the Creator to His earthly son,
Make time for Me.
You are loved and the apple of My eye,
Make time for Me.
I will build you up and make you strong,
Make time for Me.
I will guide and protect you through life's trials,
Make time for Me.
I will love you forever unconditionally,
Make time for Me.
I will give you spiritual boldness to walk righteously,
Make time for Me.
When attacked by the enemy's darts, I will be your shield,
Make time for Me.
I will provide a way of escape and wipe away your tears,
Make time for Me.
You will never be lonely, for I'll provide all your needs,
Make time for Me.
I will never leave you or forsake you,
Make time for Me.

Said the son to his earthly father,
Make time for me.
I need your love and to know I'm special,
Make time for me.
Please build me up as only a father can,
Make time for me.
I need you to direct and guide me to become a man,
Make time for me.
I need to know you love me always and unconditionally,
Make time for me.
Teach me spiritual boldness in righteousness,
Make time for me.
You are my protector when bullies try to attack me,
Make time for me.
You will make me safe and alleviate all my fears,
Make time for me.

I will never be lonely for your words will comfort me,
Make time for me.
I'll remember your words and how much you value me,
Make time for me.
I'll share the Creator's love with mine, as you did me,
Make time for me.
I will honor you and my mother, your queen,
Make time for me.
You will never be left alone or forsaken by me,
Make time for me.
The greatest gift from my Creator is my dad who will,
Make time for me.

FORGIVE ME FATHER

Forgive me Father,
Yes, I am the one,
I am the sinner,
Who crucified Your Son.

Forgive me Father,
For what I have done,
I was lied to and tricked,
By the deceitful one.

Now I am wiser,
Ever trusting in You,
Help me to forgive myself,
And become brand new.

You are forgiving,
You're merciful and just,
You are the Living,
Of Whom I've become just.

Justified in You, Father,
Justified in You, I must,
Justified in You, forever,
Justified in You, I trust!

DAD

Did your father care for you,
Was he there when you needed his hand,
Was he around to lift you up,
When you were trying your best to stand?

Did you long for his embrace,
The warmth of knowing he was near,
Were you lonely those days and nights,
And prayed for a loving father who cared?

Did your father talk to you,
Did he show you the world through his eyes,
Did he share his dreams with you,
So your mental muscles could be strong and wise?

When you made youthful mistakes,
Did your father listen with loving ears,
Or were his lectures so intolerant and cruel,
A grown man would've been brought to tears?

Did your father see your innocent face,
And value you as his precious son,
Was his time spent with valued friends,
While good times with you still haven't come?

Did your father hold you close,
Or did he beat you like he didn't care,
Did he show compassion for you,
Or expected things of you he never shared?

Did he make you feel so stressed,
You felt you hated him and yourself?
If only he would hug and say he loves you,
I know you would forgive everything else.

Dad, you are always kind and considerate,
You value me and speak words that uplift,
Always stating how proud I make you feel,
But being a great dad is also how you healed.

THE HAND OF YAHWEH

I love seeing Yahweh's hand at work,
He sets the stars and sun in space,
And made the earth our dwelling place,
I love it when Yahweh shows His hand.

I love seeing Yahweh's hand at work,
He works creatively in our lives,
And helps us not to sin or compromise,
I love it when Yahweh shows His hand.

I love seeing Yahweh's hand at work,
He orders our daily prayerful steps,
And changes our plan even if we get upset,
I love it when Yahweh shows His hand.

I love seeing Yahweh's hand at work,
He draws our hearts to comfort and cheer,
And frees us from all sin and fear,
I love it when Yahweh shows His hand.

I love seeing Yahweh's hand at work,
He strengthens our faith in ways unheard,
As we willingly obey His holy word,
I love it when Yahweh shows His hand.

I love seeing Yahweh's hand at work,
He lifts us up when we fall down,
And provides when friends are not around,
I love it when Yahweh shows His hand.

I love seeing Yahweh's hand at work,
He anoints his children to do extraordinary things,
That they're often surprised to be gifted in,
I love it when Yahweh shows His hand.

I love seeing Yahweh's hand at work,
He blesses his children as an act of love,
Sending guardian angels to protect from above,
I love it when Yahweh shows His hand.

I love seeing Yahweh's hand a work,
He draws us tenderly with compassion and care,
And makes us secure just knowing He's near,
I love it when Yahweh shows His hand.

I love seeing Yahweh's hand at work,
He's near during times of persecution and strife,
And when we're in pain or lose our earthly life,
I love it when Yahweh shows His hand.

I love seeing Yahweh's hand at work,
He changes the mind of our enemies,
Confuses those that war against His family,
I love it when Yahweh shows His hand.

I love seeing Yahweh's hand at work,
He's near when there's a flood or storm,
And in the calm or twilight of the morn,
I love it when Yahweh shows His hand.

I love seeing Yahweh's hand at work,
He gives us life after our new birth,
And prepares us for His second coming to earth,
I love it when Yahweh shows His hand.

I love seeing Yahweh's hand at work,
He's the awesome Creator of everything,
And whatever He does is for our glorious gain,
I love it when Yahweh shows His hand.

Yes, I love it when Yahweh shows His mighty hand.

WHISPER

Whisper to me Father,
Whisper in my ear,
Help me to hear Your words,
Gentle, soft and clear.

Whisper to me Father,
Let me know Your truths,
That I not be guided,
By lies that others use.

Whisper to me Father,
Guide my writing hands,
Let the words I speak to others,
Come directly as You command.

Whisper to me Father,
Your love is genuine and true,
There is no greater love than,
Love freely given by You.

Whisper to me Father,
Give us peace and rest,
Knowing good things will come,
When we trust You for our best.

Whisper to me Father,
When I dream about Your word,
Share the keys to Your kingdom,
That the world has never heard.

Whisper to me Father,
Open Your children's eyes,
Give wisdom and discernment,
That salvation will be the prize.

Whisper to me Father,
You are the very best,
Gather all your children,
To in Your presence, rest.

LILY OF THE VALLEY
(Women's Ministry)

Lily of the Valley Women's Ministry,
Is committed to reflect the Savior's love,
By the power of His Holy Spirit,
We embrace our cultural diversity,
Uniting our faith, talents, resources, and prayers,
In service that others may know our Savior cares.

Unique is each, "lily of the valley,"
Blessed to have been chosen and redeemed,
As virtuous women uplifting our Savior,
Whether we're prayer partners,
Or a part of the hospitality team,
His love through us is seen.

We are mothers, daughters, sisters, and friends,
Vowing to proclaim the Savior's love,
Uplifting each other in prayerful communion,
Obeying the commandments and lessons in union,
Trusting the Savior's light in us shines bright,
That hearts we touch will yield to His Holy light.

It's not our will, but the will of the Holy Spirit,
That dwells in each "lily of the valley,"
The Savior provides us with no greater gift,
Than our service to others that uplifts,
Our Savior's salvation is absolutely free,
And drawing closer to Him satisfies everyone's needs.

A JUST WORLD?

Is this a just world?
Where babies are dying,
Where children are crying,
Where women are misunderstood,
Where some people are heartless,
Where some leaders are thoughtless,
Where love means not what it should,
Is this a just world?

Is this a just world?
Where pockets of the rich are constantly filled,
Where government sedates the population with pills,
Where policies are not for the majorities' good,
Benefits the wealthy and not the average neighborhood,
Is this a just world?

Is this a just world?
Where there are wars and rumor of wars,
Where the innocent are dying by the score,
Where multitude of soldiers are unnecessarily killed,
And hearts of loved ones cannot be comforted or healed,
Where leaders are heartless seeking personal gain,
Where hearts of grieving families are continuously in pain,
Where they speak of peace but run to have war,
Where they joke of wealth as if poverty is a forgotten sore,
Is this a just world?
You tell me...is this a just World?

GIVE ME A VOICE

Give me a voice,
To tell of Your greatness.
Give me a voice,
That others may hear.
Give me a voice,
Of compassion and boldness.
Give me a voice,
To alleviate Your children's fears.

Give me a voice,
As I follow Your leading.
Give me a voice,
To share the words You say.
Give me a voice,
That Your children will follow.
Give me a voice,
So they will walk in Your ways.

Give me a voice,
Sharing Your love for all sinners.
Give me a voice,
Telling of the mercies You've shared.
Give me a voice,
Proclaiming the sins You've forgiven.
Give me a voice,
Showing You're a Father who cares.

Give me a voice,
Encouraging Your children to triumph.
Give me a voice,
Inspiring Your children to lead.
Give me a voice,
Telling of Your heavenly mansions,
Give me a voice,
Proclaiming Your love throughout eternity.

GRACE

A virtuous woman,
Loving and true,
Kind and gentle,
Perfectly renewed.

Generous and caring,
Always lending a hand,
Prayed for forgiveness,
Of each and every man.

The mother of many,
Selflessly loving her own,
A true giving example,
From the Almighty's throne.

Witnessed her praying,
With her husband on their knees,
Soliciting the Creator's help,
When attacked by Satan's deeds.

A faithful and loving wife,
Her husband's right hand,
She is a true example,
Of a good gift to her man.

Some may not understand,
Just how she made it through,
The enemy constantly attacks,
When he knows Yahweh loves you.

But that does not stop her,
She works from dawn until night,
Saving souls for the kingdom,
For this is her plight.

BEWARE!

Beware of those that teach you lies,
For their own selfish gain,
They'll fill you full of promises,
That will cause you so much pain.

Beware of those that smile and say,
Your sins are harmless deeds,
But when you need their comfort,
They are nowhere to be seen.

Beware of the pretenders,
Who lead sincere folks astray,
Pretenders that love to teach,
The Creator doesn't mean what He say.

The Creator is the only way,
The truth our guiding light,
When your heart reaches out to Him,
No one can remove you from His sight.

Beware of seeking wisdom,
Contrary to the way of the cross,
Seek knowledge and understanding,
And He will restore what you've lost.

Beware of seeking only gifts,
This world could satisfy,
When seeking first the Father's kingdom,
These and more He will provide.

CHOOSING BATTLES TO WIN THE WAR

She knew him years ago,
When he was not a threat to her livelihood,
Her boyfriend would pick her up,
The group met and bowled in the neighborhood.

Later needing a job, she joined his company,
Friends were happy he rose close to the top,
He was in charge of her section,
Her immediate supervisor was the cream of the crop.

With her immediate supervisor's promotion,
She had another supervisor she couldn't respect,
Who thought everything was a joke,
Lacking backbone, consistency and tact.

He called them into his office,
Talking about the work that was done,
Was pleased with what she was doing,
Then switched his conversation to a personal one.

She tried to be diplomatic,
Saying she was not trying to offend,
Her choice was to not date married men,
But maintain professionalism and respect as friends.

The more she resisted his advances,
The more determined he was to have his way,
As a ploy to get her into his office,
He would have them report about their day.

Another day they were called into his office,
The supervisor said he had another appointment and left,
He ignored her refusals to put ointment on his back,
Feeling uncomfortable, she hurriedly dabbed it on and left.

There were two young men in her life,
She was determined to keep on the narrow and strait,
An aging parent needing her more than ever,
A thesis to complete in order to graduate.

With these three battles constantly before her,
She now had a problem with this fourth,
And fighting off a selfish, lustful predator,
She hoped to resolve diplomatically and avoid the court.

She had to choose her battles and prayed this would end,
The more she resisted his advances, the bolder he became,
Being there for her family and completing personal goals,
Were her priorities and not buckling to his selfish games.

After work one night he followed her home,
Inquiring...which she tactfully refused and verbally prayed,
Time and rejections to visit her home made him bolder,
So she sought counsel from an aunt a few miles away.

Finally came to a head that he lost his harassing schemes,
As he insisted on picking her up for a legitimate job event,
He arrived, met her parent and off they went,
And directing him from her home, he changed his intent.

He immediately mentioned going to a hotel instead,
At that point she said make a right turn down the road,
And then a u-turn, and a few minutes later,
They were back in front of her abode.

Said she would meet him at their work event,
As she exited his vehicle to his surprise,
He questioned what her parent would say,
Since they had just left and said their goodbyes.

Said he was important and had somewhere else to be,
Was the answer she gave him as she walked away free,
Angry and tired seeing the harassment escalate with time,
She was firm to deal with the consequences he'd feed.

She entered her house that night and never ventured out,
When returning to work, she knew the battle was on,
Defied his sexual attempts and his pride wouldn't recoil,
How could she resist his power and he be scorned?

She knew the fight was on and prayed to her Father above,
Her defying his aggressions, made him cunningly mad,
With this final bold rejection and not achieving his goal,
She knew her existence on the job would become quite bad.

She shared her problem with a colleague,
After observing said he could see her plight,
Though her colleague could see what was happening,
She pondered to fight this battle and seek legal advice.

He gave her position to her namesake,
And behind steel bars she was placed,
Had the joker to say her work was lackluster,
Just to humiliate and put her working reputation at stake.

In answer to prayer she was delivered from his hands,
When he saw she was leaving his control,
He asked her to accept a position of another man,
She refused his offer for another job she would behold.

A co-worker at another site was going through the same,
She empathized with her and sent an encouraging card,
Watching Anita Hill on the tube, she understood the fight,
To fight this battle which priority would she disregard?

A court battle could affect her young men's stability,
Her aging parent was sick, frail and more in need,
As she diligently worked full-time on her degree,
Which battles were most important for her to achieve?

Deciding to choose this harassment battle to win the war,
Would probably have been successfully achieved,
But fighting this battle and jeopardizing the other three,
Was an inopportune time for this fight to conceive.

Years later they both attended a meeting,
When he walked in she felt resentment in her heart,
Though she'd forgiven him, knew it was time to confront,
Release her resentment for an emotionally new start.

As he was leaving the meeting,
She confronted him in the hall,
And told him how he had made her work miserable,
By his sexual harassment and unjust gall.

She told him she forgave him,
He acted like he didn't understand,
Yet he apologized for any actions,
He may have done to cause her pain at his hand.

She successfully reared two responsible young men,
Was there for a parent in need,
Completed her degree in the time allotted,
Though difficult, these were her best battle choices indeed.

UNCONDITIONAL LOVE

Have you ever known unconditional love?
Some say it's like beating the slots,
To know you are loved no matter the cost,
Is a feeling that nothing else can top.

Have you ever known unconditional love?
Let me tell you just how it feels,
To know you can make silly or major mistakes,
And another's respect for you stays real.

Have you ever known unconditional love?
Some say they'll love you as long as they live,
Although they are now nowhere around,
Their imperfect love you must forgive to heal.

Have you ever known unconditional love?
Cards may flood your mailbox from the start,
But when the honeymoon period was past,
Their action does not reveal what they ought.

Have you ever known unconditional love?
Heard it's a priceless gift to have around,
To know that you can feel secure and free,
But when needed it cannot be found.

Have you ever known unconditional love?
Are they near when you're sick and in pain,
They may go to the store for pain relievers,
But are they near as your strength is regained?

Have you ever known unconditional love?
May say they'll always be faithful and true,
The promises they make turn to silly mistakes,
Self-gratifications dictated their own rules.

Have you ever known unconditional love?
Their true love you trusted could heal,
But when you made your own mistakes,
Their love for you could not be revealed.

Have you ever known unconditional love?
You realized their love wasn't sound,
When needed to be loved for just being yourself,
It was too much intimacy for them to have around.

Have you ever known unconditional love?
Though you sought it throughout your life.
You often tested and it was hard to believe,
Love could overlook imperfections and strife.

Have you ever known unconditional love?
You gravitated to the Creator for dear life,
He showed you His love in action and words,
That unconditional love is what He's all about.

Have you ever known unconditional love?
You tested the Creator's love as you've done others,
He only showed compassion and grace,
Assuring He'd never give you up for another.

JUST KNEEL AND PRAY

When you're feeling really low,
And there's nowhere else for you to go,
Just kneel and pray.

When disappointments come your way,
And your loved ones strip your faith,
Just kneel and pray.

Do not keep those thoughts alive,
Thinking about who hurt or made you cry,
The Savior is always by your side,
Just kneel and pray.

When you believe in the Heavenly King,
Don't be surprised seeing adversities,
You must go through the trail of tears,
To find your strength in Him.

For Yahshua is our example,
And lived His Father's earthly command,
And His love for us never changes,
He'll protect us with the strength of His hands.

We can never be separated,
From the love of our awesome Creator,
He will strengthen, shield and protect us,
Even when we've gone astray.

Our Savior lived among us,
To reveal the true character of His Father,
Exposing Satan's purpose to destroy us,
Because we're the apple of the Creator's eye.

For we wrestles not against flesh and blood
There's a spiritual warfare in each of us,
The choice to yield to the one we serve,
Reveals the one we truly love.

Don't be double minded in your actions,
Trying alone to do what's right,
Pray and allow the Savior to help you,
He'll stand before your enemies and fight.

When we walk through the valley of death,
Fear shall not be on our breath,
For we know our Savior is near,
And will keep us safely in His care.

There is only one answer above.
When we go through trials in life,
Don't give in and don't give up,
Just kneel and pray.

When we lean on the Creator's hand,
And trust His son to do what we can't,
The Holy Spirit will lift us up,
When we just, kneel and pray.

MY GIRLS

You are my precious diamonds,
From the moments you were born,
I sent up prayers to heaven,
Giving thanks for the birth of my jewels.

Yet how would you know your value,
Except it comes from me,
The way a father treats you,
Nothing less from a mate you'll receive.

I strive to be an example,
Of a father's love and care,
Your mother simply adores me,
I praise her for the wisdom she shares.

I'm affectionate with my daughters,
Faithful and loving to my wife,
To be respected and loved by my family,
What a great and gifted life.

Your mother and I were excited,
The year your double-digit age arrived,
We wanted the experience to be lasting,
Our father-daughter date was your surprise.

You are treated like a princess,
With my time, love and respect,
You know how much I adore you,
And won't allow others to respect you less.

You look to me for guidance,
Your earthly father of love,
I read scriptures to you at bedtime,
My heart melts with your cuddly hugs.

How priceless are my angels,
As you sleep in peace and rest,

I kneel and ask my Creator,
Guide me to be my best.

You awake in the dawn of the morning,
With the voices of loving songs,
We sing Psalm 91 for protection,
As we welcome our Creator at dawn.

He sends His angles to protect us,
Because we love Him so,
We know and will honor His holy name,
And make sure Yahweh's name is known.

Purity in spirit is how we must be,
We send up prayers like kisses on bended knees,
As our Creator supplies our daily needs,
We strive to be there for our family.

Whatever trials may come our way,
We'll dwell on joy and laughter,
Things may not always be perfect in this world,
But prayerfully, we'll live happily ever after.

PROACTIVE

The times we spend with the ones we love,
Increases our own vitality,
When we make conscious choices to do unto others,
Those choices become our own reality.

It's easy to find more important things to do,
Less complicated to just do what we please,
It's the gift of giving cheerfully to others,
That helps others to truly believe.

True lessons in life are not what we say,
That makes another feel we'll be there,
Words become weightless when our action seem to fail,
For it's what we do that proves we genuinely care.

Whether it's a father, mother, sister or brother,
Our children, friends or relations,
When we exercise our words when another's in need,
There should be no hesitation.

It's a good thing to depend on oneself,
But we were not created alone,
What makes one truly fulfilled and complete,
Is building a solid and supportive home.

Time is so precious yet fleeting,
We've been given one body, one voice,
Remember to use them wisely,
And consciously stay on our course.

INTEGRITY

Are you a person of integrity,
Or hide behind masks of deception and greed?
Will you tell lies for personal gain,
So others will think you've earned that claim?
Are you obsessed with wares for others to see,
Just to be accepted in their fake society?

Will you be truthful when keeping your word,
Or say you don't recall if a witness never heard?
Will you agree to one thing and do another,
Not caring if it offends a partner or a brother?
Do you treat the needy with hospitality and respect,
Or will they be treated like unwelcome guests?

Will you embrace the affluent and discard the poor,
Placing spreads before the rich you eagerly afford?
Will you ask the loaner to forgive the loss,
When you have ample means to repay the cost?
Are you eager to listen when others communicate,
Just to hear their concerns to selfishly manipulate?

The only things you will carry into eternity,
Are your character, a good name and bold honesty.
The toys and things gathered will soon be lost,
When death speaks, true character will pay the cost.
Will you do wrong when you should do right,
Just to feel superior to others during this earthly fight?

I hope not,
Because I can clearly see,
For my character,
And my name is,
Integrity.

"DON'T FLY IN THE FACE OF GOD"

Said the child to her dear mother,
Questioning things that happened in her world,
"Why, why, why did God?"
The questions flowed,
The child asked more,
She had so many questions why?

The mother responded with loving sternness,
"Don't fly in the face of God.
His plans or His methods or,
His purpose for your life,
Is only for Him to decide."

The mother was firm to trust and obey,
Leaving her concerns on the altar as she prayed,
She learned through her lineage,
To pray, trust, and obey,
Knowing all things worked for her good.

As the child returned to question why,
Her mother would take her aside,
They would pray together,
During calm or stormy weather,
Yet the mother was consistent in her ways.

The mother responded with loving sternness,
"Don't fly in the face of God.
His plans or His methods or,
His purpose for your life,
Is only for Him to decide."

The years passed, as did her mother,
Yet, she was blessed to learn this lesson well,
"Because His plans or His methods or,
His purpose for your life,
Is only for Him to decide,
Don't fly in the face of God."

SERVICE

When we are young,
We learn our chores,
Washing the dishes,
And dusting the floors,
We learn to pray,
And tried to obey,
Things our parents taught us,
Each and every day.

When we venture in the world,
For work or college,
The lessons we learned,
Increases our knowledge,
Yet that is good,
But with all that,
We need understanding,
To stay on track.

When we marry,
And leave our homes,
We serve our mates,
In ways unknown,
We may have children,
To shower with hugs,
But the greatest gift to give them,
Is to teach the Father's love.

When we're no longer,
Together with our mates,
Through relational hardships,
Or death that we hate,
Be prayerful, stay focused,
Be humble and request,
Our Creator to strengthen us,
As He redirect our steps.

Our Heavenly Father,
Shields us from negative forces,
When we seek Him first,
He hears our prayerful voices,
And He knows each journey,
We all must take,
The battles that's before us,
Is to strengthen our faith.

Commit to serve Him,
In our words and in our deeds,
Forsake all earthly things,
That pulls us from praying knees,
Be steadfast and committed,
Our work is not in vain,
We will be rewarded,
If we trust Him and never faint.

DESIRE

I desire to please You,
I desire to one day see You,
I desire to walk the paths You've laid,
I desire to witness to YHWH's glorious name,
That's My Desire.

I desire to serve You, throughout this life,
I desire to nurture others by Your Holy insights,
I desire to expound on Your faithful truths,
I desire to illuminate Your word giving no excuse,
That's My Desire.

I desire to teach the young and old,
I desire Yahshua's keys to release the captured souls,
I desire to explain biblical truths unclearly heard,
I desire to turn Satan's counterfeits into stupid verbs,
That's My Desire.

I desire to exalt Your Holy Name,
I desire to remember Your Sabbath's blessed claim,
I desire to share Your lessons in elementary term,
I desire to see others boldly study to learn,
That's My Desire.

I desire to inspire all to seek Your face,
I desire for all to be drawn into Your Holy embrace,
I desire to see the veil removed from their eyes,
I desire them to know love and obedience wins the prize,
That's My Desire.

A RIGHTEOUS MAN

I've been trusting and praying for the man of my dreams,
Have chosen before making wrong decisions it seem.
Only My Creator can lead the heart of the right man,
I want not my own will, but my Creator's righteous plan.

He called Mother's Day sending wishes that I enjoyed,
Only heard his voice a few times in the years before.
My heart was elated the memories flew back,
Yet we were not equally yoked by the Creator in the past.

Father, only You can change the heart of a man,
You've changed me and all my old selfish plans.
As emotionally high as I felt at that time,
A few moments later reality settled my mind.

It was good to be thought of, a kind jester too,
But hearing his voice was like a whisper from You.
We have both grown older, but were we both wise?
I want a righteous mate and the temptation made me sigh.

I talked to my Creator saying not my will but Yours,
My past decisions failed, Your will is what I'm praying for.
I don't want him Father if he is not a gift from you,
I'm here to be a blessing to others wanting a husband too.

With experience and maturity and times of fallen hopes,
I quietly and trustingly look to my Father to pull my ropes.
I then went to dinner with other empty nest mothers,
We enjoyed the meal and stories of our children and others.

And leaving the restaurant a gentleman in a suit spoke,
He stared remembering where together we had worked.
As my sister friends and I were talking in the parking lot,
He acknowledged me by name as he drove off.

He took his mother to dinner this special Mother's Day,
I guess that was his son too, but he didn't bother to say.
Why did the first man call and why did the other stare?
I only know my Creator will guide me through my prayers.

I pray for a righteous man after my Creator's own heart,
With just that one request, we'll never be spiritually apart.
The Creator holds the chord uniting a husband and wife,
As they prosper and share loving examples in this life.

He knows who will trust Him and what tomorrow holds,
I pray for the desire of His heart for the man I shall behold.
All of us must trust Him to give us the desire of our hearts,
As we humbly seek and never from our Creator depart.

Personal choice for a husband may not always be the best,
Responsibly trust and obey as He gives us our daily tests.

THEY TALKED ALL NIGHT

A week ago he called and said,
"Good morning,
Have a blessed day, and
I will always love you."

Awakened by his strong voice,
She suddenly sat upright in her bed,
As she dwelled on his words,
His voice had been eternally etched in her mind.

A soft tear escaped and cooled her cheek,
As her heart leaped inside,
Her mind had recorded his every word,
She was shocked into a joyful mood.

What prompted this outbreak,
He had been restrained so, so long,
What was he actually saying,
Could years of separated love last this long?

As the years past he was always in her heart,
His phone number she could still recall,
In earlier days he was stable and she was carefree,
That was no surprise, he was older you see.

Her grandmother thought he was the best,
He would joke and say she was his girlfriend,
She knew he would be good for her,
And fondly asked about him through the years.

In those years they were strongly attracted,
And some times they passionately disagreed,
He said she captured his heart as he did hers,
And he wanted to marry.

This was a different kind of love for her,
Something she had never experienced in the past,
He's was a practical and romantic country guy,
Who knew what he wanted and wanted this to last.

She had begun a career and was self-sufficient,
Could she leave and trust him to protect and care,
Could this strong willed independent woman,
Not be rejected later on through the years?

Their marriage never happened,
They went their separate ways,
They seldom talked through the years,
Yet their love and emotional stability stayed.

She knew he was in a safe place in her heart,
A place locked safely were she could visit at will,
She knew how she felt about him,
And was at peace if he no longer felt the same.

Years later she called hoping to hear his voice,
To let him know her grandmother passed away,
And a secret desire to talk like good friends again,
But their conversation was like that of distant friends.

He was charming and they bid each other goodbye,
He called a month later and shared greetings for that time,
A month later she called him to share the same,
As he called another time, he realized she was in pain.

That's why it shocked her so,
That day he called her on the phone,
She believed he no longer loved her,
But the words he shared were what she felt for him.

When a week ago he called and said,
"Good morning,
Have a blessed day, and
I will always love you."

A week later she called him again,
Acknowledging she would be a minute on the phone,
It was late in the evening,
But their conversation lasted until dawn.

This man she always enjoyed talking to,
Who had never been few with words,
Filled up her emotional love cup that evening,
And explained his love for her never waned.

He said it didn't matter where they were in life,
He only wanted what was best for her,
If he had to he would give her up a thousand times,
His gift of love was allowing her to be free.

She doesn't know what the future holds,
Will neither ask nor hope for what may never be,
She's just at peace knowing she was deeply loved,
And the love was in unison between he and she.

And though she often prays for him,
Hoping for his spiritual growth and success,
She can finally say they are now truly friends,
And wish him years of peace and happiness.

Truly blessed to have talked to her dear friend,
What a joy in her heart it was,
The evening when they talked all night,
Was prompted by touching words of his love.

When a week ago he called and said,
"Good morning,
Have a blessed day, and
I will always love you."

NO EARTHLY GOOD

To be told you're so heavenly minded,
That you're no earthly good,
May be stated tactfully in love by others,
Should you change to act like you're from the hood?
Heavens no!

Often your conversations relate about heavenly things,
When blessings abound you credit to the Creator's hand,
Should you say blessings are the birthright of men,
Acting like the crowd just to be a part of their plan?
Heavens no!

Your journey is to strive towards the heavenly kingdom,
Although earth is the narrow road you're passing through,
Should you feel ashamed that your head's in the clouds,
Doing just what you were created on this earth to do?
Heavens no!

People are caught up in the world's distractions,
Yet you are not oblivious when things happen around you,
Others think the urgent salvation message isn't cool,
Should you put blinders on and act as they do?
Heavens no!

You may hear the voice of a different drummer,
Your actions are the result of the words you believe,
People are really watching to see if you're consistent,
Should your actions change during times of trial or grief?
Heavens no!

All of heaven is watching to help each soul you reach,
Harvest is full awaiting your opportunity to speak,
Will you be quiet when you may be the last one they'll seek,
Allowing your fears to control what you do, say, or think?
HEAVENS NO!

A SISTER

A sister is a welcomed friend,
She'll stick with you through thick and thin,
When you accomplish goals in life,
She's there to celebrate with much delight.

She'll lift your spirit in words and deeds,
Knowing all things work for good as we believe,
She's not competitive when you achieve,
But hopes you're happy as you succeed.

Your girl-time secrets are safe with her,
Her confidence is not lost with gossiping words,
And when sick, she'll lovingly nurse you to health,
For her love for her sister is beyond material wealth.

She fears the Creator and trusts in His name,
She's truthful in all the things that she claims,
Her virtue is never compromised,
For she trusts the Creator to continually guide.

NEVER TOO LATE

Those early years were built,
On love's youthful expectations,
They went off and married,
Lacking maturity to guide their way.

It wasn't long before,
They reached their own limitations,
Looking to find their happiness,
Through the love of their insecure mate.

They were selfish in giving to the other,
Immaturity and pride prevented harmony,
Each one acted uncaring towards the other,
Justifying their personal and selfish needs.

Soon it was too late for them to see.
The rafters of their foundation couldn't breath,
They looked to the other to satisfy every need.
With this strain their marriage could not succeed.

Apart and alone,
They wished for new romance,
They were no longer together,
And both prayed for a second chance.

They were opened to learn,
Seeking guidance from the written Word,
By allowing older couples to teach them,
And the Holy Spirit to guide, they heard.

They learned their lessons well and,
Became prayerful, loving and mature,
Remarried each other, the love of their life,
To enjoy a foundation made spiritually secured.

FAITH

I have faith to cast down mountains,
I have faith to still the sea,
I have faith to walk on water,
I have faith the Savior died for me.

My faith grows when reading the Bible,
My faith grows by meditating on His word,
My faith grows as He fulfills each promise,
My faith grows seeing the future as His past tense verb.

My faith is strengthened with each new trial,
My faith is strengthened with past victories,
My faith is strengthened by the love He showers,
My faith is strengthened as prayers become realities.

My faith is steadfast to always please Him,
My faith is steadfast to trust when I can't see,
My faith is steadfast believing His promises,
My faith is steadfast because His Holy Spirit is in me.

I have faith in my loving Father YHWH,
I have faith in His precious Son Yahshua,
I have faith in the guidance of His Holy Spirit,
I have faith knowing my salvation has been won.

VIOLA

A grandmother full of laughter,
A grandmother filled with joy,
A grandmother never judgmental,
A grandmother with open doors.

A grandmother who would listen,
A grandmother with sound recall,
A grandmother who lived a Christian life,
During the summer, winter, spring and fall.

A grandmother who was caring,
And always prayed for me,
Although she's no longer living,
Her prayers encompass eternity.

I AM MERCIFUL

When you decide to turn from sin,
And you want Me to enter within,
I am merciful.

When your life is in despair,
And it seems like no one cares,
I am merciful.

When you pray for a child that's lost,
And wonder if I hear your thoughts,
I am merciful.

When unable to provide for your needs,
And you want Me to intercede,
I am merciful.

When your ways please Me,
<u>Ask</u> anything,
<u>Believe</u>,
And you shall <u>Receive</u>,
For I Am Merciful.

REDEEMED BY LOVE

Born in a life of poverty,
Thought nothing was special about the name she received,
Lost a sibling before he entered elementary,
Sent to live with strangers that treated them mean.

Although obedient was not appreciated,
Degraded continually and treated with hatred,
Physical beatings were a daily thing,
Verbal put downs caused far more mental pain.

Though slapped and beaten was forced not to cry,
Went to church on Sundays, and weekly living a lie,
Church on Sunday and hell the other six,
How could they have survived that crazy lunatic?

Experienced first-hand what slaves went through,
Ironing cords showed backs of black and blue,
Eight years old and the eldest of two,
Had no one to talk to nor knew just what to do.

Weapons of assaults were a cut garden hose or a board,
Like cattle sometimes the abuser tied them to a door,
Locked her refrigerator with lock and key,
If hungry they waited until she felt it was time to feed.

The abuser talked to friends about how bad they'd been,
Suggested they be placed in ice water as a punishment,
Freezing them for hours she didn't care it wasn't right,
She doted on her grandson she adored day and night.

Divided and conquered to make them hate themselves,
No one to nurture them they were fearful and distressed,
Their nerves were stressed working from morning to night,
Awakened at night to redo chores not done, "just right."

So much happened don't have time to tell,
But years later, she was strong enough to run like hell,
Left that place and told everything to authorities,
They did absolutely nothing but placed her in another family.

The abuse through the years caused many tears to flow,
Sharing the pain with others may have cushioned the blows,
It took her time to even stop wetting the bed,
Difficult to trust because of the abuse done to their heads.

Failed the first year of high school due to poor study habits,
The new home was better thought she was in heaven,
The abuser called the home she was happily adjusting in,
Told lies of how bad a person she, "supposedly" been.

Since adults don't think other adults will lie,
The abuser's words were repeated causing tears to fly,
Felt unprotected, unshielded, unloved and wronged,
The year there was better, but had enough and was gone.

Moved in with her dad and older siblings,
Excelled in classes and several after school teams,
Her self-esteem was low but fought to build it up,
Disallowed descending remarks, was confident in herself.

As time went on, had a child and marriage,
Marriage ended but motherhood strengthened her courage,
Strong enough to refuse staying in an abusive situation,
To live like the past, she definitely had no patience.

Without a mother's guide mistakes were made,
Divinely protected though suffered as children each day,
Grew to know the Creator and how His Son paid the cost,
He'll redeem all suffering and sadness the abuser brought.

Learned to love her Father through the written Word,
She can tell you of His love and the healing of her hurts,
As He showed His matchless love in words and in deeds,
She knows His unfailing love's the greatest gift received.

RESTORER

Our Creator is a restorer,
A restorer of broken families,
A restorer of abandoned friends,
A restorer of broken relationships,
A restorer of dishonorable men,
A restorer of women to virtue,
A restorer of honor to parents,
A restorer of sad and broken hearts,
A restorer from anguish and pain,
A restorer from selfish pleasures,
A restorer from selfish gains,
A restorer from sinful bondage,
A restorer from prison gangs,
A restorer from sin that's binding,
A restorer from jealousy and hate,
A restorer from self-mutilations,
A restorer from conceit and distaste,
A restorer from prideful behavior,
A restorer from envy and deceit,
A restorer from being ungrateful,
A restorer from having no peace,
A restorer when seeking our purpose,
A restorer to be humble and complete,
A restorer to abandon our idols,
A restorer to forgive others gracefully,
A restorer when we desire salvation,
A restorer from prodigals to kin,
A restorer of desire to search scriptures,
A restorer of our love to commune with Him,
A restorer when we desire to seek His face,
A restorer of our trust in Him to wait,
A restorer when we ask to increase our faith.
He restores us to His heavenly place.
Our Creator is a restorer.

TREES OF RIGHTEOUSNESS

Trees of Righteousness,
Our Savior and healing friend,
A role model who taught truth and love,
What an exemplary life He lived,

Trees of Righteousness,
We are His many branches,
As we trust in the Savior's love,
We escape Satan's sinful distractions.

Trees of Righteous,
For everyone who accept and believe,
He is our road map of joy and peace,
As we plant His spiritual seeds.

Trees of Righteous,
We are to preach good tidings to the meek,
And with His words to open blind eyes,
We're to comfort the broken hearted and weak.

Trees of Righteousness,
Proclaiming liberty to captives bound in sin,
As He calls us to open the prison doors,
In the day of vengeance sorrow become grins.

Trees of Righteousness,
Who'll give beauty for ashes of shame,
He'll give oil of joy for their mourning,
And all burdens will be clothed with praise.

Trees of Righteousness,
He invites us to enter the gates with thanksgiving
For our labor on earth will soon be over,
As we look forward to our new beginnings.

EPITOME OF ME

The words, "I Love You,"
Comes as easily as the,
Air you breathe,
The euphoric feeling of sensational charges,
Erupts into a glow seen by others just looking at you,
You are in love,
But are you?

Love says, I will never leave nor forsake you,
Love says, I will provide for you,
Love says, not just for now, but always,
Love says, I forgive you and wish only life's best for you,
Love says, I will love you beyond the end of this world,
Mankind won't always love you,
But I will.

I love you,
Man, woman, boy and girl,
And after you have learned how to love,
From all the princes of false philosophies,
I will draw you lovingly back to Me,
And, I will give My love,
Visions for you to see.

You are My beloved,
And because I love you,
I will teach you love's true meaning,
Without any need for apologies,
For love's,
True essence is,
The epitome of Me.

D'LEIGH

I can see my sister's love for you,
Not in what she'll say but what she'll do,
She's not preachy when others come to pray,
She'll just hold your hand along life's way.

She is sensitive, a loving work of art,
Who tirelessly gives from the wealth of her heart,
She takes care of others before her own needs,
For she values a friend beyond what others can see.

But don't think she's weak,
To be humble and meek,
These are gifts of the Holy Spirit,
That in all people, our Creator seeks.

She will fight and cry for others,
She's the cream of the crop,
When others need compassion,
She's on the list at the very top.

You are blessed to have known her,
She is blessed with the renewal of a friend,
You're both honored to spend this time together,
As spiritual sisters and best friends once again.

When asked if she talked to you about salvation,
And giving your heart to the Savior this day,
She said others have come to pray for you,
Though suggested her duty is to share it anyway.

She went about the business,
Of loving you through her deeds,
When the doctor said you can eat and do anything,
She accommodated your requests and your needs.

And when she told me you requested,
Her to take you to a church the following week,
It was evident that you witnessed the Savior's love,
Through her actions and not words she may have preached.

For it is in wisdom that we embody the Creator,
When we nurture bodily needs that others seek,
Some will preach until the coming of the Savior,
Yet not a saved soul will their preaching reap.

I am proud to have D'Leigh as my sister,
Knowing she is holding your weak and frail hands,
She must have a star in the heavenly kingdom,
For her love in action, is showing you, the Promise Land.

TELL IT

There's a song that says
"Go tell it on the mountain,
Over the hills and everywhere,"
Yahweh admonishes us to
Go tell our stories,
Let His words echo everywhere,
That people may know His love.

So don't be shy,
Do what you must,
Share the good news,
Our Savior is just,
Share your stories,
Share your cares,
The Creator is with us,
Everywhere.

"Your Family"

Daily Affirmation

Most Precious Loving Father, YHWH,

(Insert your family name), **our children and grandchildren throughout all generations, affirm that the windows of Heaven are opened to us, our loved ones, families and spiritual mates, right now to provide us with an abundance of Wisdom, Discernment and Understanding from You.**

Blessed Father and Creator Yahweh, we claim upright and honorable spiritual relationships with You by our prayers, our actions, our words, and our deeds. We claim excellent health, wealth, love, family relationships, protection, friendships and Your wonderful blessings in all areas of our lives, including *(insert- school/occupation/business, etc.)*, **and in all other areas of prosperity that You, Father Yahweh, manifest to Your glory.**

We thank You Almighty Father, for the immediate manifestation of Your blessings, which we humbly accept, and boldly go forth and accomplish, right now, by Your grace, our awesome Father and Creator Yahweh, in Your Son, Yahshua's holy and precious name we pray, Amen.

SECTION 3

"Let him that boasts boast about this: that he understands and knows Me, that I am Yahweh, who exercises kindness, justice and righteousness on earth, for in these I delight," declares Yahweh.

Jeremiah 9:24

BIBLICAL TRUTHS

**"Reading the Bible converts the heart
To do the Father's will,
Seeking wisdom by studying,
Makes us blessed and spiritually fulfilled."**

Abby Gail

ALL

All My commandments you shall observe and do,
For in them you will have life,
Your family will multiply and possess the land,
I swore to your fathers during their lives,
My commandments were given to bless you,
To keep you in right standing with Me,
They are not impossible for you to keep,
When you trust Me to strengthen your belief.

My words are sharper than any two edged sword,
They will guide all who seek Me earnestly,
Desiring and doing what I command,
Fulfills you in ways you can't conceive,
Some think it's impossible to be righteous,
In your own strength it is difficult you see,
Your righteousness is as filthy rags,
Yet, a righteous person I command you to be.

To be righteous is to yield to and love the Creator,
Who knows your imperfections yet loves you still,
King David was a man after the Creator's heart,
Though he sinned he became justified and forgiven,
David acknowledged his sins before the Creator,
Each time he humbled himself and wept,
The Creator knew the heart of this dear man,
He'd forgiven and counted as righteous.

We look at each other and see our sins,
But we don't know the heart of any man,
When we look for friends or select a spouse,
We'll make mistakes if our trust is not in Him,
So seek Him first, His kingdom and righteousness,
And He will choose righteous people in your life,
Don't be concerned when you're called to be righteous,
Without His grace we could not win this spiritual fight.

Our Creator knows the sincere person,
One who will strengthen your spiritual life,
Although you may want to do the right thing,
Selfish desires causes conflict and strife,
Our Savior has already paid the cost,
At the cross we were given the victory,
When we do His commands and seek His face,
Righteous children will be our destiny.

Even when our flesh is weak,
He is our shield and buckler,
He strengthens us and judges our hearts,
To become righteous gifts to others,
If we sin and fall short of the Creator's will,
And seek Him in sorrow and humility,
He said though a righteous man falls seven times,
He is considered righteous because he trusts in Me.

FROM THE HEART OF A CHILD
"The Lord's Prayer"

Almighty Father,
Holy and Righteous is Your name,
May Your kingdom come,
Down to this earth.

May Your desires,
Be done on the earth,
Like it is done in Heaven.

Heavenly Father,
Please give us this day,
Our daily food and shelter.

And forgive our sins,
As we forgive
Others who sin against us.

Let us not be tempted,
To do things displeasing You,
And deliver us from wickedness,
Pain, harm, and misery.

For You created the kingdom,
You have all power,
And deserve all the glory,
Forever and ever,
Amen.

THE PRODIGAL

There once was a father,
Who had two loving sons,
He doted on them like royalty,
And withheld nothing good from either one.

The eldest was contented,
To labor each day for his dad,
The younger dreamed of better things,
Far away and different from what his father had.

The father was a wealthy man,
Had servants working his house and the land,
The servants were totally happy there,
Because the father was an honest and righteous man.

One day the youngest son,
Decided he just had to go and see,
This world he knew was boring to him,
He wanted to feel alive and free.

He could not wait to spend his wealth,
Through wastefulness and reckless extravagance,
He wanted to experience what the world was like,
New friends, forbidden appetites and finally this chance.

He asked his father for his inheritance,
He knew his dad would not deny,
He happily left his wealthy homeland,
Yet, he didn't notice the tear in his father's eye.

Imagine how the father ached for his son,
Gazing down the trail each night and day,
Longing and hoping his son would return,
Not to reprimand, but hug him and celebrate his stay.

The prodigal had a gay old time,
Recklessly spending the money he received,
He satisfied his appetite with many forbidden things,
With his wealth spent, friends were nowhere to be seen.

He was broke, sad, hungry and alone,
Found a job feeding a herd of pigs,
Yet no one bothered nor cared about his needs,
So-called friends were out doing their own gigs.

He thought to himself questioning his plight,
Why am I in misery with no food and stressed,
There was no one he could call on to shelter him,
Even the pigs were content while he was under duress.

His meager salary didn't stretch through the month,
There must be a lesson in this he finally confessed,
It was senseless to stay here in this predicament,
His father's servants are treated fair and given respect.

With only the clothes he had on his back,
He started towards his father's house,
He thought he'd ask to be his father's servant,
He felt unworthy to return and was filled with doubt.

He felt guilty as he saw his father running towards him,
Filled with a mixture of emotions was sad yet relieved,
How could his father run to him with open arms?
His father's wonderful behavior was a relief to see.

His father hugged and kissed his neck,
As the prodigal confessed his unworthiness,
He offered to gladly work as his hired servant,
Knowing the grief his father endured by his selfishness.

The father draped his son in a royal robe,
And ordered a feast fit for a king,
His long lost son had returned safely home,
And he wasted no time letting the celebration ring.

The father had all he ever wanted from his child,
Which was for him to come back to the fold,
When this one lost sheep was gone astray,
The family was not quite whole.

The celebration had been going on for a while,
When the older brother returned to their house,
He inquired what was going on inside,
As a servant informed him in joyful shouts.

He was surprised, amazed, shocked and angered,
To see his brother celebrated this day,
While he worked all along and obeyed his dad,
Not one time was he celebrated this way.

The father approached the older brother,
And invited him to come inside,
As the older son spoke of his anger and resentment,
The father encouraged him to understand his side.

The father said you were always with me,
And everything I have is yours,
Your brother was lost but now is found,
Open your heart and allow our family to be restored.

MY BLESSED 90%

As we write this check before we rest,
We want to say thank You Father,
As we share what we have to help others,
Giving to those in need is in actuality,
Giving back to our Heavenly King,
Before we start another day,
We want to say, thank You Father.

We enjoy the shades from Your trees,
The grass, the cool breeze,
Your many gifts we reflect,
Your special day of rest,
And all Your blessed benefits,
As we write this check before we rest,
We want to say, thank You Father.

You asked us to return only one-tenth,
From jobs, skills or gifts we've been blessed with,
That your gospel of love may continue to spread,
Reaching hearts of those that would otherwise be dead,
We are chosen as co-laborers for Your kingdom,
As we write this check before we rest,
We want to say, thank You Father.

You're not like the government,
With taxes that constantly rise,
Your one-tenth has never been upsized,
You promised to bless the 90% we have left,
When we joyfully relinquish Your ten percent,
As we write this check before we rest,
We want to say, thank You Father.

Oh how blessed it is to return what is Yours,
It's a privilege to be trusted with this awesome reward,
For everything we have is totally Yours,
It's an honor to be a member of Your family,
That Your gifts to us will set all men free,
As we write this check before we rest,
We humbly say, thank You Father.

YOU LIED

Jealous and insecure,
Wealthy but poor,
Popular but friendless,
Intelligent but stupid,
Privileged but cheats,
Ability but mediocrity,
Free but enslaved,
Ability to heal but kills.

Don't blame me,
Didn't suck up to your priorities,
Prayers and wise choices set us free,
Granted wisdom and understanding,
Of the Creator's superior abilities.

Your lies will be revealed,
For the entire world to see,
With every truth the Creator reveal,
You substituted with lying counterfeits,
The world will be amazed when they see,
You burn in hell's inferno.

You lied to the world,
As you slivered like a snake,
Your end is near,
And the Creator will not wait!

TRUST

It is written to, "Trust no man,"
So how do we manage our days?
With every decision and choice made,
Our trust must always be in Him.

Our Savior sees the heart of man,
And knows who will seek Him first,
It's unwise to partner with unlike minds,
Seek His guidance to fulfill your thirst.

Ask the Savior to be your guide,
Read the scripture and pray,
Wisdom is seeking counsel,
As the Holy Spirit guide the way.

It is written to, "Trust no man,"
Yet Abraham was a man of faith,
Willing to give his son to the Creator,
Was an act of putting Him first.

When Isaac was eligible to marry,
Abraham sent his servant to find a wife,
And before the servant finished praying,
Rebekah responded to his prayerful delight.

The scripture gives examples,
How trusting others paid the cost,
By relying on their own understanding,
The price was pain or material loss.

In the story of the Garden of Eden,
Adam trusted Eve, who trusted the snake,
When asked by the Creator about their sin,
Blamed the woman He gave, for the mistake.

Remember the twin Esau and Jacob,
Jacob coveted the birthright of his brother,
To receive Esau's birthright blessing,
Deceived his blind and dying father.

Sampson trusted his lover Delilah,
With deceit obtained the secret of his strength,
Cunningly she revealed to soldiers as he slept,
Who conquered and made him an embarrassment.

Foolish Nabal trusted in his wealth,
He arrogantly mistreated King David's men,
As the king advanced to slaughter his household,
Yahweh interceded by the humble plea of his kin.

It is written to, "Trust no man,"
For the Savior is ready to guide,
For every decision take time to pray,
That choices you make will be wise.

UNEQUALLY YOKED

We rear our children to do the Father's will,
We teach and preach hoping morals are instilled,
With words of wisdom taken from the holy book,
We pray they'll take the straight and narrow course.

We pray they'll be determine and wise,
Only seeking friendships of like minds,
For they've been taught not to be yoked,
With individuals determined to act like dopes.

Father, how can they grow,
When they put their trust in man,
The answer's not with these simple foes,
But is defined in Your written plan.

Some may think its funny,
But they'll have a price to pay,
Don't listen to the voice of others,
That will steer your good sense away.

To co-mingle with others,
Who follow a different drummer,
Can steal your existence,
For a peaceful and brighter tomorrow.

Except the Creator build your house,
Your friendships or marriage will be in vain,
To be unequally yoked with unbelievers,
Will cause you years of misery and shame.

So don't think you know,
More than the Creator does,
Seek His face, trust His word,
And be enveloped in His awesome love.

APPOINTMENTS

You think I've received this appointment,
Because of underhanded deals or my looks,
Prayer and preparation afforded me this opportunity,
And I strive to practice what's in the Creator's book.

You want to believe as the carnal minded do,
The unpopular should not be elevated above you,
You think the righteous should remain subordinate,
Which makes no sense to anyone but a fool.

Appointments are given to the righteous,
And appointments are given to the wicked,
There's a purpose for every appointment,
But some minds are filled with jealousy and sickness.

Choices are made by each and every person,
The Creator sees the heart of every man,
We may live like there is no tomorrow,
Time after time our acts reveal His master plan.

Some may ask, do we have a choice?
Doesn't matter what people will do,
The Creator knows everyone's decisions,
And will use our choices as His tool.

It's up to every one of us,
To choose to do evil or good,
No matter how we paint the canvas,
His purpose in the end will be just what it should.

Appointments are given to kings and men,
Pharaoh thought he was in total control,
The choice was in his powerful two hands,
First he refused to let the Hebrew slaves go.

Pharaoh freed the slaves then had a change of heart,
His decision was reversed due to pride and selfish gain,
His army chased after the slaves and into water was lost,
His greed and unwise choice determined his ultimate pain.

The Bible tells how Joseph suffered for many years,
He learned to lead others by being an honorable man,
He lived obediently through many trials and tears,
To be appointed to the second highest position in the land.

The righteous pray for appointments and wait,
Which should be of no concern to man,
Knowing the Creator makes no mistakes,
The final choice is always in His righteous hands.

WOMAN OF VIRTUE

To be a woman of virtue,
In today's society,
Is difficult to envision,
Without praying constantly.

There're so many distractions,
Her work, friends, or T V,
But she is strong and determined,
To honor her Creator and family.

Proverbs says, it is difficult to find her,
For her price is extremely high,
She costs much more than rubies,
This woman of virtue is dynamite.

She strengthens herself each morning,
She prays on bended knees,
Reads and knows the scriptures,
To sustain her spiritually.

Her husband trusts her implicitly,
All she does is for his good,
Unlike others that ruin their husbands,
Her man is respected in the neighborhood.

She's adored by her husband,
And is fulfilled in his loving arms,
They make time together in the evenings,
To converse and plan for another dawn.

She clothes her household properly,
Selects diligently when she shop,
She's a knowledgeable investor,
And makes prudent land deals buying lots.

Her garden is full of vegetables and fruits,
She prepares and stores food for later use,
She replenishes her pantry when items get low,
And cooks for her family and unexpected souls.

She reaches out to help people in need,
And gives food and clothes to the poor,
She comforts the sick and diseased,
Speaking words of wisdom, kindness and more.

She often wears the color purple,
And looks sleek in the color of royalty,
Doesn't worry when the snow is heavy,
She has prepared warm coats for her family.

She is honest when working with others,
Is creative in selling her wares,
Ensures her household is doing well,
And waste no time in idle cares.

Her children grow up and bless her,
Her husband exalts and praises her too,
There are other women of virtue,
But she excels, heads above the few.

Many women may be favored,
But even this, a man can not trust,
And some women of beauty and vanity,
When love is captured, are idle and selfish.

My son, seek and find a woman of virtue,
A woman who fears and honors Yahweh,
And if she's endowed with beauty, that's OK,
She'll make your life and home a haven of praise.

The fruit of her hands will show her work,
Her work will praise her in your home,
Blessed is the man who finds her,
A virtuous woman who cares for her own.

ISN'T IT WONDERFUL!

Isn't it wonderful,
That we can do,
A greater work than our Savior,
Isn't it wonderful,
That we can be used,
When we give our Creator all,
He will use us when we call,
No matter how many times we fall,
Isn't it wonderful,
Isn't it wonderful!

Isn't it wonderful,
That we can do,
A greater work than our Savior,
Isn't it wonderful,
That we can be used,
When we give our Creator all,
He will guide our willing hands,
When we yield to His perfect plan,
Isn't it wonderful,
Isn't it wonderful!

Isn't it wonderful to know,
He used our fathers and our mothers,
Isn't it wonderful to know,
That He still cares,
When we're weak and in despair,
He can use us even there,
Isn't it wonderful,
Isn't it wonderful!

He used King David,
Who committed murder and adultery,
He used a child name Joseph,
Hated by his siblings and abused,
As Joseph was imprisoned in Egypt's jail,
The Creator used him even there,
Isn't it wonderful,
Isn't it wonderful!

The Savior used the woman,
Who was caught in adultery,
When no stones were cast,
He said, go and sin no more,
There are other people I could name,
Still He used them just the same,
What He has done for them,
He'll do greater works through you.

Isn't it wonderful,
That we can do,
A greater work than our Savior,
Isn't it wonderful,
That we can be used,
When we give our Creator all,
If you think you're so low in sin,
Just remember he's even used the dead,
As he called Lazarus from the grave,
He's calling you.

Isn't it wonderful,
That we can do,
A greater work than our Savior,
Isn't it wonderful,
That we can be used,
When we give our Creator all,
He has laid His redemption plan,
And uses every woman, child, and man,
Who have faith in Him,
And allows Him to guide them through.

Isn't it wonderful,
That we can do,
A greater work than our Savior,
Isn't it wonderful,
That we can be used,
When we give our Creator all,
For every work our Savior did,
Glorified the Father,
Whose DNA He has,
And as sinful and forgiven souls,
We may do greater works than He.

Isn't it wonderful,
That we can do,
A greater work than our Savior,
Isn't it wonderful,
That we can be used,
When we give our Creator all,
Although we are sinners in this land,
Our sinless Creator incorporates us in His plan,
Though we're not face to face with Him,
Our Savior intercedes for His own.

Isn't it wonderful,
That we can do,
A greater work than our Savior,
Isn't it wonderful,
That we can be used,
When we give our Creator all,
The greater works that we shall do,
When asked in the Savior's name,
The Father shall do,
That the Father may be glorified in the Son.

Isn't it wonderful,
That we can do,
A greater work than our Savior,
Isn't it wonderful,
That we can be used,

When we, give our Creator all,
Not just for others that you've seen,
But for everyone who truly believes,
Isn't it wonderful,
Isn't it wonderful,
Isn't it wonderful!

HEAVEN

Heaven is a real place,
Prepared for you and me,
To live with our Creator,
Throughout eternity.

Don't know the day or hour,
Our Savior will return,
But hold onto His promise,
And live what you have learned.

Don't listen to false prophets,
That say He's here or there,
The same way He left this earth,
In like manner He shall appear.

His appearing will be visible,
And every eye shall see Him,
With angels in the clouds of glory,
To change His own to immortal beings.

Even the blind will look up,
And see the brightened sky,
As lightening circle the globe,
His brilliance is seen as wide.

He's coming with authority,
It will be intensely loud,
Piercing sound of thunder,
That awakes death in the ground.

All the graves will open,
The dead in Yahshua will rise,
Then all the saints living,
Will join His angels in the sky.

They'll be with their Savior,
That special and glorious day,
The wedding feast is ready,
The bride is on her way.

They'll sing halleluYah,
Salvation, glory and power,
All belongs to our Savior,
Who freed the saints this hour.

Yahweh cast down Satan,
Who corrupted mankind,
Deceiving many nations,
And mocking the Divine.

Woe to those who shun Him,
With more important things to do,
Now pleading as molten elements,
Destroys the earth now doomed.

For the time to repent is over,
Opportunities have been tossed,
The Creator said it is finished,
You're in the Book of Life or lost.

All will bow to the Savior,
And acknowledge His royalty,
His mercy and His kindness,
Redeemed for all to see.

Those that followed Satan,
And trusted his device,
Will agonize for losing,
Salvation that cost no price.

If you deny the Bible,
Being wrong is a heavy cost,
He knows your inner makings,
And gave all to prevent your loss.

The Creator made us different,
We may not always clearly see,
We're given freedom of choice,
Use butterfly faith and believe.

Don't act like you're embarrassed,
Be as the woman with tears and oil,
Who humbly washed Yahshua's feet,
For life that's free and unsoiled.

Heaven is a real place,
The Savior shared the scene,
He will guide us safely home,
To peace and serenity.

New Jerusalem is marvelous,
The streets are paved in gold,
Wisdom beyond imagination,
Where we will forever grow.

Take our Savior's loving hands,
Give yourself permission to go,
And if you're awaiting His return,
Heaven promise you joys untold.

NOTES

NOTES

SCRIPTURES

Worship Me (Exodus 20:1-6)
Splendor of His Name (Exodus 20:7)
Remember (Exodus 20-8-11)
Honor Your Father and Mother (Exodus 20:12)
Do Not Murder (Exodus 20:13)
Adultery (Exodus 20:14)
Stealing (Exodus 20:15)
Don't Lie (Exodus 20:16; Revelations 21:8)
False Witness (Exodus 20:16)
Longings (Exodus 20:17)
It's Not About Me (Deuteronomy 8:1-20)
All (Deuteronomy Chapter 8)
From the Heart of a Child (Matthews 6:9-13)
The Prodigal (Luke 15:11-32)
My Blessed 90% (Malachi 3:8-12)
You Lied (Revelations 20:14)
Trust (Psalms 146:3; Jeremiah 9:4;)
Unequally Yoked (Psalms 127; II Cor.6:14)
Appointments (Exodus Chapters 12-14; Gen. 41)
Woman of Virtue (Proverbs 31:10-31)
Isn't It Wonderful! (John 14:12-13)
Heaven (John 14:1-3; Revelations)

REFERENCES

Holy Bible, King James Version: (Oral Roberts Evangelistic Association, Inc., 1981)

Mom's Devotional Bible, New International Version: (Zondervan Publishing House, 1966)

Restoration of Original Sacred Name Bible: (Basis of the Rotherham Version, 1976, Revised by Missionary Dispensary Bible Research, 5th Edition 1977)

The Sacred Scriptures: Bethel Edition, Premier Publication: (Assemblies of Yahweh, 1981)

The Old Testament of the Jerusalem Bible: (Darton, Longman & Todd, Ltd. and Doubleday & Company, Inc. 1966)

Strong's Exhaustive Concordance of the Bible: James Strong, S.T.D., LL.D.: (Mac Donald Publishing Company)

New World Dictionary of the American Language, Student Edition: (William Collins & World Publishing Co., Inc.) Presented by Time, Webster's New Ideal Dictionary: (G. & C. Merriam Co., 1968, 1973)

Our Times and Their Meaning, Carlyle B. Haynes: (Southern Publishing Association, 1929)

INDEX OF POEMS

Printed in the United States
122591LV00003B/191-610/P

9 781604 778557